✠ THE BOOK OF ✠
SAINTS

Rodney Castleden

Quercus

CONTENTS

INTRODUCTION

The word 'Saint' is a derivation of 'Sanctus', a Latin word meaning 'sacred', and it is used to describe a person who has lived an exemplary life of great charity and virtue; someone who has committed themselves to the cause of Christianity and contributed to its progression, and who, in the eyes of the Catholic Church and popular opinion, is to be considered holy.

Such a person officially becomes a Saint after the process of canonization. This is a long investigation into their life, their achievements, and the miracles which they performed. Miracles, especially those which occurred after their death, contribute greatly to the elevation of their status.

Although canonization can take many years, even centuries now, attaining sainthood in the early days of Christianity was a less formal process. Prominent missionaries, especially those who died for their faith, were often canonized, and often straight away. As were those who led con-spicuously virtuous lives, and who were, in effect, an example to other Christians by imitating Christ. People became saints through public acclamation – with the accolade coming shortly after, sometimes immediately after, they died.

As the middle ages wore on, formal rules regarding canonization were introduced. One miraculous cure at the grave of a deceased person was not sufficient cause for canonization; several were needed, and the people who claimed them were subject to interview by Church authorities, who wanted to verify the claims.

Today, the process is even more complicated and extremely formal. Since the rules were formalized by the Catholic Church in 1983, it has been necessary to wait at least five years after the person's death before the process can even begin. Then the bishop of the diocese opens an investigation, enquiring into the person's specific Christian virtues – faith, hope, charity, prudence, justice, temperance and fortitude. If this enquiry shows them to be worthy, he or she is honoured with the title Servant of God. Then the case goes before the Congregation for the Causes of Saints. If the Congregation can be persuaded that miracles have occurred, the candidate is beatified and honoured with the title Blessed. After that process is completed, another miracle must occur before the title Saint can be conferred.

The 100 saints who appear in this book lived in different centuries, and came from different walks of life and parts of the world. They inevitably reflect the values of their own times and backgrounds, but they share one thing: they have risen far above ordinariness, achieved something very remarkable and wonderful, and become shining examples to other human beings.

St Hilary

Chronicle

BORN
Poitiers, France

DIED
368 of natural causes

PATRONAGE
Against snakes, backward children, snake bites

MEMORIAL
13 January, formerly 14 January

PRAYER
When I look at your heavens, according to my own lights, with these weak eyes of mine, I am certain with reservation that they are your heavens. The stars circle in the heavens, reappear year after year, each with a function and service to fulfil. And though I do not understand them, I know that you, O God, are in them.

Hilary was born in Poitiers in the fourth century. He was brought up as a pagan and was an adult convert to Christianity. He appears to have been chosen as Bishop of Poitiers before he was even ordained priest; he was even married with a daughter, Abra, at the time when he became bishop, but lived a celibate life from that time on. Like Ambrose and Cyprian, Hilary was made a bishop by public acclamation.

Hilary became famous as a teacher, with a reputation as a fluent and articulate speaker, a 'Rhone of eloquence'. The young St Martin went to Poitiers to hear him, and became his disciple. Hilary became chiefly known for his opposition to the Arians, to whom he appeared a formidable opponent. The Emperor Constantius, who was strongly influenced by the Arians, banished Hilary to Phrygia in 356. There he wrote a commentary on the Psalms as well as letters to his family, including one to his daughter Abra encouraging her to refuse an offer of marriage and instead consecrate her life to the service of God, yet at the same time leaving her free to choose. He was a strenuous arguer, but also courteous and a believer in tolerance. Abra followed her father's wishes, but died shortly after his return to France four years later.

In 363 he travelled to Italy, where he held a public debate with Auxentius, the Arian Bishop of Milan.

Hilary died in 368 after a lifetime defending the Christian faith in public debate and in his many writings.

St Anthony
(the Great) of Egypt

Born of wealthy Egyptian parents in AD 251, Anthony was inspired soon after his parents' death to give his substantial legacy to the poor. From then on he led a strict ascetic existence, eating only once a day and drinking only water.

Perhaps because of the lifestyle of deprivation and austerity he imposed on himself, Anthony was plagued by phantoms in the form of beautiful women. These were interpreted as temptations by the Devil. He withdrew to the desert and lived in a pit, into which his friends lowered food. In his pit it was believed that Anthony spent his time battling with his demons.

A cult developed, and others followed his example. The desert was colonised by hermit monks, and Anthony governed them like a benign abbot. Visitors to his retreat always recognised him by the extraordinary beauty and cheerfulness of his face. Occasionally he left the desert to preach in Alexandria, but it was from the desert that he drew his strength, and he was never away from it for long. He explained his need to return to the solitude of the desert by comparing himself to a fish out of water, 'Fish die if they lie long on the dry land.'

Anthony died at the age of 105 in AD 356. Athanasius said that Anthony was like a physician given by God to Egypt; 'Who met him grieving and did not go away rejoicing? Who came full of anger and was not turned to kindness? Who came troubled by doubt, and failed to gain peace of mind?'

St Wulfstan

Wulfstan was born in 1009, the son of a Warwickshire thane, and he was to become the last of the Anglo-Saxon saints. He was a strikingly good-looking man with an engaging manner; he was fond of social life and all kinds of sports and games, and as a youth had no intention of entering the Church. It was possibly the example of his parents that swayed him. They both renounced the world in their old age, retiring to the cloister, and perhaps visiting them in their religious community showed him the merits of this very different, alternative way of life.

Wulfstan spent 25 years in a monastery at Worcester, where he rose to be prior. His new lifestyle was a complete contrast to his earlier life, and he loved to preach to the poor, in spite of the custom that monks should not preach. As Bishop of Worcester he acted like a shepherd with his flock. He loved children and people brought their infants from far and wide to be baptised by Bishop Wulfstan.

He was a great builder of churches, but his real love was for people, not buildings. When the new cathedral at Worcester was completed, he exclaimed in tears, 'The saintly men of olden times cared more to bring their flocks to God than to build fine churches. All we do is to raise piles of stones; for souls we care nothing.'

After William of Normandy's conquest of England, Wulfstan's career in the Church was almost cut short. He was despised at court as a yokel; he was far too homely and unpolished for the Norman courtiers. The new king himself said in plain terms, 'Wulfstan is a fool. He cannot speak French.' William's Archbishop, Lanfranc, tried to depose Wulfstan on the grounds that he was incompetent. Wulfstan was summoned to Westminster to answer the case against him. He fell asleep while his adversary was making the case 'for the prosecution'. Wulfstan disarmingly admitted that he was unworthy to hold office, went to the tomb of Edward the Confessor and laid his staff upon it. The staff remained fixed and unmovable on the tomb. It was said that neither the King nor his Archbishop could move it. Only Wulfstan himself was able to pick it up again. Thanks to this miracle the sentence of deposition was rescinded. The story may be apocryphal, but somehow Wulfstan succeeded in persuading the Norman officials in Westminster that he should remain bishop.

He was restored to his bishopric and became Lanfranc's friend, helping him to suppress the Irish slave trade, which had developed strong links with the port of Bristol. Wulfstan went to Bristol to talk directly to the traders, preaching to them every week in their own language. As a result, the slave trade came to an end. Wulfstan died in 1095 aged 86. He was a fundamentally good and kind man, modest, questioning and self-effacing.

✝ Chronicle ✝

BORN
c.1009 at Icentum (now Long Itchington), Warwickshire, England

DIED
Wulfstan died in 1095 while engaged in the daily ritual of washing the feet of a dozen poor men

CANONIZED
14 May 1203 by Pope Innocent III

MEMORIAL
19 January

REMEMBRANCE
The Great Malvern Priory was founded by St Wulfstan and he was also responsible for a large amount of rebuilding work carried out to Hereford Cathedral, Worcester Cathedral and Tewkesbury Abbey, as well as many other churches in the same area. There is a commemorative altar in the Great Malvern Priory which is dedicated to St Wulfstan alongside that of King Edward the Confessor.

St Sebastian

Sebastian was born and brought up in the north Italian city of Milan. He was a Christian, but in spite of this he rose to the rank of tribune in the Roman army, commanding the first cohort at Milan.

Sebastian encouraged two waverers to stand by their Christian faith instead of denying it. It was not long before he was denounced to the emperor, who tried to reason with him. When he found that Sebastian could not be swayed, he ordered that he should be shot to death with arrows. Sebastian was tied to a tree and shot through many times and the archers left him for dead. At nightfall, a devout woman called Irene came to untie him, bind up the wounds and revive him. He gradually made a complete recovery.

When he was well enough, he decided to confront the emperor, telling him that his priests were false and that Christians were not enemies of the state. The emperor was furious at this impertinence and ordered Sebastian to be beaten to death with sticks. His body was then thrown into the city's main drain, where it was found by another Christian matron, Lucina, who had his body buried in the catacombs. There, on the Appian Way, they later built the basilica of St Sebastian, a favourite focus for pilgrimage in the middle ages. Sebastian was a popular saint; prayers addressed to him were thought to be effective against the plague.

Chronicle

BORN
Narbonne, Gaul

DIED
Martyred *c.*288 at Rome

PATRONAGE
Archers, armourers, arrowsmiths, athletes, bookbinders, diseased cattle, dying people, enemies of religion, fletchers, gardeners, iron mongers, lacemakers, laceworkers, lead workers, masons, plague, police, soldiers, stone masons and stonecutters

MEMORIAL
20 January

PRAYER
O Lord, grant us a spirit of strength. Taught by the glorious example of Your martyr, Saint Sebastian, may we learn to obey You rather than men. Amen

St Agnes

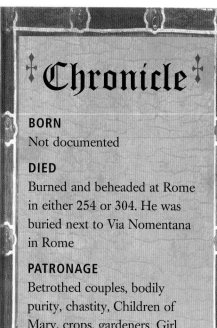

✦ Chronicle ✦

BORN

Not documented

DIED

Burned and beheaded at Rome in either 254 or 304. He was buried next to Via Nomentana in Rome

PATRONAGE

Betrothed couples, bodily purity, chastity, Children of Mary, crops, gardeners, Girl Scouts, girls, rape victims, virgins

PRAYER

All-powerful and ever-living God, You choose the weak in this world to confound the powerful. When we celebrate the memory of Saint Agnes, may we like her remain constant in our faith. Amen.

Very little is known about the personality or actions of St Agnes, though she was held in the very highest esteem by such men as Prudentius, St Jerome and St Ambrose. St Jerome wrote of her, 'In the writings and tongues of all nations, the life of Agnes is praised in the churches, the blessed martyr Agnes, who overcame her own youth and the tyrant and consecrated her chastity by martyrdom.'

Agnes was the daughter of an aristocratic and wealthy Roman family and she was brought up as a devout Christian. Then, when she was just thirteen, the son of the governor of Rome fell in love with her. He asked her parents' permission to marry her, but they respected Agnes's wishes and asked for a delay. The suitor persisted, but Agnes answered that she had already given her heart to Christ. 'Such is his beauty that the brightness excels all the brightness of the sun and the stars; the heavens are ravished with his glory. He is so powerful that all the forces of heaven and earth cannot conquer him. I love him more than my soul and life and am willing to die for him.'

At this the suitor became bitter and angry. His father, Sempronius, intervened; he too tried to persuade the girl to change her mind. When he failed and in the process discovered that Agnes was a Christian, Sempronius saw a way of exacting revenge without appearing to be pursuing a personal issue. He summoned her before a tribunal and ordered her to marry or to become a Vestal virgin: 'Sacrifice to the goddess Vesta, and serve all your life among the virgins who keep the sacred fire for Rome.' Still Agnes refused to co-operate.

Then the governor's son had a convulsion and fell as if dead at her

feet. Sempronius was distraught, accusing Agnes of sorcery. Agnes told Sempronius that it was an act of God, and she prayed for the young man to be returned to life. He revived, and Sempronius was so grateful that he would gladly have reprieved Agnes, but by now a wave of popular anger had risen against her. She was a sorceress and had to be executed.

Agnes was placed on a pyre, but the flames encircled her like a rainbow and blazed out, consuming the executioner's assistants. Eventually the executioner beheaded her.

The Christians of Rome buried Agnes in a catacomb that still bears her name, in the Via Nomentana. Her parents prayed at her grave continuously for a week until a day when they witnessed a company of virgins dressed in cloth of gold and crowned with garlands. In the middle of them was their daughter with a white lamb at her side. She told her parents not to weep but to be happy for her.

The Emperor Constantine built a basilica on the site of her martyrdom outside the walls of Rome, close to the Porta Pia.

St Vincent

Chronicle

BORN
At Heusca

DIED
Martyred *c.*304 at Valencia

PATRONAGE
Vine dressers, vinegar makers, vintners, wine growers, wine makers

REPRESENTATION
He is often depicted as a deacon holding a book or a ewer and a book. He can also be seen with ravens or holding a millstone.

PRAYER
Holy God, Saint Vincent served You as a permanent deacon and gave his whole life and soul to You, even to the point of becoming a martyr . . .

Vincent was a Spaniard, a native of Saragossa, and he was born in the late third century. He was educated by Valerius, the Bishop of Saragossa, who made him first deacon and then archdeacon. Valerius delegated the task of teaching to Vincent as he himself suffered from a speech impediment.

At that time, Spain was a province of the Roman Empire. The Governor of Spain was Dacian and he became responsible for implementing the edict of the Emperors Diocletian and Maximus, under which the Christians were to be persecuted. In AD 304 Dacian accordingly had both Valerius and Vincent seized and taken to Valencia for questioning.

Valerius was sent into exile, but Vincent was, unfairly, kept for much harsher treatment. He was tortured on the rack and his flesh was ripped with iron hooks; he was laid on red-hot bars. It made no difference to Vincent's resolve. He said, 'You see how the tortured is stronger than the torturer!' He was taken back to his cell and made to lie on pieces of broken pottery. That night, his gaoler looked into his cell and was astonished to see it filled with angels and lit with a heavenly light; Vincent himself was singing hymns with the angels. The gaoler was instantly converted by the sight.

After this, Dacian relented and handed Vincent over to his friends. Unfortunately, Vincent died of his injuries almost immediately. His body was later buried under the altar of the principal church of Valencia.

scs vincenci

St Paul

St Paul is without doubt one of the most important saints in the history of Christianity. It was Paul who widened the Christian mission to include the non-Jewish communities of the Mediterranean region, and prepared the way for Christianity to become a world religion. Arguably, without Paul the teachings of Jesus would have remained of interest only to Jews, and Christianity might have been little more than an obscure Jewish sect.

Paul was born with the name Saul at Tarsus, the capital of Cilicia. His father was well off, Jewish, a member of the tribe of Benjamin, and a Roman citizen, and Saul grew up with a fierce loyalty to Jewish law and tradition. Consequently, he enthusiastically opposed the 'heretical' new sect of Christianity and joined in the persecution of St Stephen and other followers of Jesus. While he was on his way to hunt down suspected Christians in Damascus, Saul was struck blind as he heard the voice of Christ saying to him, 'Saul, Saul, why do you persecute me?' Saul was so convinced that Christ himself had appeared and spoken to him that he devoted the rest of his life to serving Christ – with immediate effect. He switched in a moment from being intent on Christianity's destruction to turning it into a world religion. This conversion (after which he was known as Paul) took place in AD 34, about a year after the Crucifixion.

Paul had to endure a great deal of persecution himself as he pursued his mission. He told the Corinthians that he had been given 39 lashes five times, been beaten with sticks on three occasions, and even been stoned. He was well aware of the extreme danger that he courted by espousing the cause of Christianity, and must be seen as one of the most courageous martyrs of all.

Paul was eventually taken to Rome as a prisoner in about AD 60. He was kept in a hired house. Though chained to his guard, he was able to write inspirational letters there to the Ephesians, Philippians, Colossians and Philemon. He was acquitted and released two years later. Then he was imprisoned once more and was entirely alone when he came to trial. He knew his time had run out. 'I have fought the good fight, I have finished the course, I have kept the faith.' Paul was beheaded in Rome, probably in AD 67.

It could be thought that Paul took over Christianity, doctored and managed its philosophy – he became its central living promoter in the generations after the death of Jesus. Yet what he did to Christianity long-term was to make Christ central to the new religion, just as the Law had been central to the old. The way that Paul had himself experienced Christ decisively moulded his view of religion; Christ could be experienced as a direct spiritual visitation that by-passed all the teachings of earlier times. It was a powerful vision and it swept the world.

St Polycarp

Chronicle

BORN

c.70

DIED

c.155 at Smyrna body burned

PATRONAGE

Against earache; dysentery

MEMORIAL

26 January

PRAYER

Lord God almighty, Father of Jesus Christ, your dear Son through whom we have come to know you, God of the angels and powers, God of all creation, God of those who live in your presence, the race of the just: I bless you. You have considered me worthy of this day and hour, worthy to be numbered with the martyrs and to drink the cup of your Anointed One, and thus to rise and live forever, body and soul, in the incorruptibility of the Holy Spirit. Amen

Born in about AD 70, Polycarp was set up as Bishop of Smyrna by Saint John. Polycarp knew not only John but others who had known Jesus. The historian Irenaeus knew Polycarp well and discussed with him what John and the other disciples had said about Jesus. When he heard strange doctrines being promoted, he would say, 'Good God, how have you made me live in times when I have to tolerate such things!' Polycarp told Marcion, whom he regarded as a heretic, that he recognised him as the firstborn of Satan.

A small amount of Polycarp's correspondence has survived.

Near the end of his life, Polycarp went to Rome when Anicetus was bishop there and conferred with him on the date of Easter. They could not agree, but remained on friendly terms.

Polycarp died during a persecution of Christians in Smyrna. He hid, but made no attempt to escape once he was discovered. He was taken before the proconsul and invited to offer sacrifice to Caesar and the Roman gods, but he refused. He had served Christ for 86 years, he said, and could not turn against him now. The proconsul threatened to have him burnt alive, but it was to no avail.

Bystanders noticed that he had difficulty in removing his boots, a task normally undertaken by a disciple. He went willingly to his death, praising God. 'I bless you that you think me worthy of the present day and hour, to join the number of the martyrs.'

St Thomas Aquinas

Thomas Aquinas was the most learned of the saints, the greatest of the so-called medieval schoolmen. Born near Aquino in Italy in 1225, he was the cousin of Frederick II. He was something of a child prodigy. His parents intended him to become the abbot of Monte Cassino, and sent him there to be educated at the age of only five.

When he was twelve he returned home, acting as his father's almoner or charity-dispenser during a famine. After that he studied at Naples, at the university just founded there by the Emperor Frederick II and became famous for his intellect. He decided to become a Dominican friar, which his parents tried hard to prevent. The Dominicans spirited him away in secret, but his brothers waylaid him on the road to Paris and he was imprisoned for two years. Eventually when he escaped his family relented, and he was allowed to become a Dominican friar.

The Dominicans sent Thomas to Cologne to study under Albertus Magnus, who mistakenly thought him stupid, nicknaming him 'the dumb Sicilian ox'. In 1248 he was, nevertheless, appointed second professor in their school at Cologne. He led a life of severe austerity. Once, while preaching on the sufferings of Christ, his description was so vivid that the sermon was interrupted by the sobs of the congregation. He soon acquired a reputation as a great preacher, lecturer and writer. He had mastered Plato, Aristotle and Arabian philosophers as well as Christian theology. He was preoccupied with his intellectual life, and sometimes forgot where he was. On one occasion he suddenly banged on the table as he shouted, 'There is an argument that will confound the Manichaeans.' Then he realised the occasion – he was dining with Louis IX, the King of France.

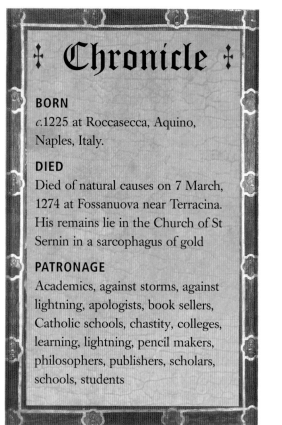

✝ Chronicle ✝

BORN

c.1225 at Roccasecca, Aquino, Naples, Italy.

DIED

Died of natural causes on 7 March, 1274 at Fossanuova near Terracina. His remains lie in the Church of St Sernin in a sarcophagus of gold

PATRONAGE

Academics, against storms, against lightning, apologists, book sellers, Catholic schools, chastity, colleges, learning, lightning, pencil makers, philosophers, publishers, scholars, schools, students

In 1261, Pope Urban IV invited Aquinas to Rome, where he began the *Summa Theologica*, which was to contain the entirety of Christian theology, including answers to all conceivable objections. This work occupied the last nine years of his life and was never finished. The project was not unlike the over-ambitious *Key to All Religions* of George Eliot's character Casaubon. Eliot may have been conscious of this parallel, as another of her characters uses Casaubon's face as a model for a portrait of Thomas Aquinas. Certainly both Aquinas and the fictitious Casaubon took themselves and their work extremely seriously.

Just before he died Thomas Aquinas had a vision while he was celebrating Mass. After that he refused to write any more, saying, 'Everything I have written seems worthless beside what I have seen.' He fell ill while travelling in 1274 and was taken to the Benedictine Abbey of Fossanuova. He died at the age of 48.

St Bridget (Bride)

✠ Chronicle ✠

BORN

453 at Faughart, County Louth, Ireland

DIED

Died of natural causes on 1 February, 523 at Kildare, Ireland. She was buried in Downpatrick, Ireland and her remains were taken to a monastery at Vadstena

CANONIZED

7 October, 1391, by Boniface IX

PATRONAGE

Babies, blacksmiths, boatmen, cattle, chicken farmers, children whose parents are not married, dairymaids, dairy workers, fugitives, infants, mariners, midwives, milk maids, newborn babies, nuns, poets, poultry farmers, poultry raisers, printing presses, sailors, scholars, travellers, watermen

NAME MEANING

fiery arrow (= brigid)

One of the patron saints of Ireland, Bridget was born at Faughart in Northern Ireland in 453. Her father was an aristocrat, but her mother was a bondmaid, not his wife. The wife was jealous and angry, selling the bondmaid and her daughter to a wizard, who brought up the child.

It was an odd upbringing, with the child teaching the foster parents and converting both the wizard and his wife to Christianity. On their conversion, they gave Bridget her freedom. She and her mother returned to Bridget's natural father, who tried to sell them off again, but when the King of Leinster discovered his reason for selling, he refused to buy. In the end, Bridget was allowed to enter the Church. She was dedicated by Bishop Mel.

After that she founded the Abbey of Kildare, a religious house for both men and women. Many miracles were reported of Bridget. Once she watched the sun setting behind the Wicklow Hills in the company of a blind nun. Bridget was sorry that her companion could not see the beautiful sight, and touched her eyes. Suddenly the blind nun could see. She turned to Bridget and asked her to close her eyes once more; 'When the world is so visible to my eyes, God is less visible to my soul.'

Bridget died at Kildare on 1 February 523. For hundreds of years afterwards, the nuns of Kildare kept a fire burning at her tomb in her memory. She also became a favourite saint in Scotland and England, where she is known by the name St Bride.

St Blaise

FEAST DAY: 3 FEBRUARY

Chronicle

BORN
Armenia

DIED
Flesh torn by iron wool-combs, then beheaded *c*.316

PATRONAGE
Wild beasts, animals, builders, carvers, construction workers, coughs, goitres, healthy throats, stonecutters, throat diseases, veterinarians, whooping cough, wool-combers and wool weavers

PRAYER
O glorious St Blaise, who by your martyrdom left to the Church a precious witness to the Faith, obtain for us the grace to preserve within ourselves this divine gift . . . You miraculously restored a little child who was at the point of death because of an affliction of the throat.

St Blaise, or Blasius, patron saint of woolcombers, was originally a kindly doctor based at Sebaste in Armenia. As a Christian missionary, he was chosen to be Bishop of Sebaste. He liked to withdraw to solitary places because of their beauty and for the company of the wild animals. Often he retired to a cave on Mount Argus, near the town. The wild animals used to gather round him, apparently waiting for his blessing. Sometimes he attended to their injuries.

He was unfortunate in living at a time of persecution under the Emperor Licinius. In AD 316 he was discovered in his cave, which attracted attention because it was surrounded by wild animals.

The Roman soldiers sent to arrest him found Blaise prepared. He said, 'Let us go at once. Today the Lord remembers me.' When he was taken before the tribunal, the governor Agricolaus greeted him: 'Hail, Blasius, favoured of the gods.' Blaise rose to the bait. 'Hail, noble prefect. They are no gods, but devils.' Agricolaus ordered him to be beaten, hoping that he would recant, but Blaise refused. The governor then had his back flayed, but Blaise only said, 'My body is in your power, but you have no power over my soul.' The governor had Blaise thrown into a lake, but he floated back to the shore radiant with dazzling light. After that, the unrelenting governor had him beheaded.

In his special relationship with the animal kingdom, Blaise is something of precursor of St Francis. In paintings, he is sometimes shown accompanied by birds bringing him food.

St Valentine

Valentine or Valentinus was a priest in Rome during the reign of Claudius II (Gothicus), who was emperor from AD 268 until 270. Valentine became well known for the conscientious way in which he cared for others. He was eventually challenged by the authorities because he was not worshipping the officially sanctioned pagan Roman gods. A judge asked him what he thought of the gods Jupiter and Mercury. Valentine said it seemed to him that they spent their time in sordid pleasures. The Emperor was impressed by Valentine's courage. When the prefect of the city saw that the Emperor might let Valentine off, he asked the Emperor if he thought they all ought to forsake the religion of their ancestors. Claudius feared that rebellion might follow, and gave Valentine up to the prefect's custody. The prefect put Valentine under house arrest in the house of one of the judges, Asterius.

Valentine and Asterius fell into conversation about the validity of Jesus's claims, and Valentine insisted that Jesus was the True Light. Asterius decided to put this to the test. He told Valentine that he had an adopted daughter who had been blind for two years. If Valentine succeeded in restoring her sight Asterius would believe in Jesus and do anything Valentine asked. The young girl was brought to Valentine, who laid his hands on her eyes. Valentine invoked the help of Jesus, and the girl's sight was miraculously restored.

Asterius and his wife threw themselves at Valentine's feet and asked what they should do. Valentine ordered them to smash all the idols they possessed, fast for three days, and then undergo baptism. Asterius and his wife and his whole household of more than forty people were baptised, and Asterius set free all the Christians.

These new Christians were soon to die for their faith. Valentine himself was thrown into a dungeon and beaten with sticks. He was killed and buried on the Via Flaminia.

A church was built to commemorate Valentine's martyrdom near the Ponte Mole in Rome, and the city gate close to this church, Porta del Popolo, was for a long time called the Gate of Valentine.

Valentine is the patron saint of young girls, but his recognition in the modern calendar as the patron saint of romance owes nothing at all to his life. The romantic association came about because of the chance coincidence between the date of his death and a pagan spring festival dedicated to the goddess Juno. This festival was for boys and girls – hence the romantic association. The early church leaders in effect adopted the pagan Roman lovers' festival and gave it Valentine's name.

St David of Wales

Little is known about St David, or Dewi, the patron saint of Wales. His mother was Irish. As a youth he studied in monastic schools founded by St Germanus of Auxerre and he was taught by Paulinus, Germanus's disciple. He presided over two synods of the Church of Wales and he founded many monasteries in southern Wales. There are legends about David – such as his pilgrimage to Jerusalem, his consecration as archbishop by the Patriarch of Jerusalem, and his father's kinship with King Arthur – but there is no evidence to corroborate them.

David led a life-long struggle against the encroaching Saxons, and against paganism and heresy amongst the Welsh. In the legends surrounding St David's turbulent life the pagan priests he confronted were often referred to as 'magi' or wizards.

A synod of Welsh bishops met to condemn heretical beliefs and then attempted to speak to a vast assembly gathered at the place that is now called Llandewi-Brevi, in Cardigan. The crowd was so huge that the dismayed bishops despaired of making themselves heard. In the end David was summoned. When he spoke his voice sounded as clearly as a trumpet and it was heard by everyone present. A white dove is said to have settled on his shoulder while he preached and the ground to have heaved up underneath his feet until it became a mountain. Later a church was founded on the spot. As a result of his effectiveness at the conference David was made Archbishop of Menevia, the modern St David's.

David may have chosen Menevia as his headquarters due to its coastal location and its accessibility from Ireland. He was interested in maintaining a close liaison with the bishops in Ireland. It was said that thirty years earlier St Patrick had stood there, deeply discouraged, and experienced a vision of the Ireland that would be won over to the Church by his own efforts. That momentous historical association may have been the real reason why David chose Menevia. Certainly it was through David's monastic institutions that the Irish and Welsh monks were especially united.

St David's monastic rule was very severe. Monks had to wear the coarsest garments, eat the simplest food and engage in hard manual work. Their intellectual life was also important, but the instant the bell rang for a service they had to break off from their reading, even if it meant leaving a sentence unfinished.

St David died at St David's on 1 March, probably in the year 601. In his last days a huge crowd gathered to receive his final blessing, and there was a great outpouring of grief at his death. It was said that older people mourned him as a brother, younger people as a father, and that kings mourned him as a judge. People cried, 'Who will teach us? Who will help us? Who will pray for us? Who will be a father to us as David was?' In fact his monasteries continued to function as sanctuaries for hunted and defeated Welsh people, and St David's became a shrine of pilgrimage.

✝ Chronicle ✝

BORN
c.542 at Menevia (now Saint David's), Wales

DIED
c.601 at Mynyw, Wales

PATRONAGE
Doves, Wales

REPRESENTATION
St David is often depicted preaching on top of a hill, with or without a dove perched on his shoulder. In the stained glass window (*far left*) he is shown holding a staff and a book

PRAYER
O Holy Spirit, Saint David received a vision from Jesus that sent him to Jerusalem where anti-Christian sentiment was strong. By relying on You, he preached so powerfully that he converted many who had been attacking the Faith. I seek his intercession for the people in my life who fight against Christian values and religion . . . Amen

St Chad

FEAST DAY: 2 MARCH

By the mid-seventh century, the impetus had gone out of the Christianisation of southern England and the missionary impulse was coming from the North, from the Celtic church so despised by Augustine, and from people like St Chad.

Chad was one of four Northumbrian brothers who all became priests after being trained by Aidan at Lindisfarne. Chad was a monk at Lastingham Abbey, where he succeeded his brother Cedd as abbot. St Wilfrid travelled to France to be consecrated Bishop of York and delayed before returning. Impatient with the delay, King Oswy selected Chad to be consecrated in his place. After his consecration, Chad set about his duties conscientiously, but when Theodore of Tarsus became Archbishop of Canterbury he visited York and told Chad that he had not been properly consecrated. Chad responded, 'I willingly resign the office, for I have never thought myself worthy of it; but though unworthy I submitted out of obedience to undertake it.' Chad was a gentle and fearful character, but spoke simply and directly. Theodore was deeply impressed by his humility and undertook his formal consecration as bishop; he nevertheless decided that Wilfrid was the rightful Bishop of York and Chad withdrew to Lastingham.

Theodore appointed Chad Bishop of the Mercians,

giving him responsibility for a huge area of northern and central England. He governed his diocese with such humility that he travelled everywhere on foot – until the Archbishop intervened, personally forcing him onto a horse. By this time, Theodore had come to recognise that Chad was an unusually holy man.

Chad built himself a little oratory near the church, where he retreated with eight monks whenever he had time to read and pray, but he had only two more years of life left. One day his disciple, Owini, who had been the chamberlain and councillor to Queen Ethledreda, was working outside when he heard the sound of a choir singing sweetly and descending from Heaven. It came from the south-east, moved to the oratory and then seemed to come from inside it. After half an hour it came out and went back up into the sky. Owini went into the oratory; Chad asked him to summon the eight monks. When they arrived, he asked them to go to the church and ask the rest of the brothers to pray for him, because he was to die. When the monks departed, Owini stayed behind to ask Chad about the singing. Chad was startled and said, 'If you heard the heavenly company, you must promise to tell no-one what you heard until after my death. They were angels who came to call me to Heaven, and they promised to return in seven days to take me away with them.'

Chad fell ill and died seven days later, on 2 March 672. Bede, writing not long after, described his tomb as a wooden structure built like a little house, with a hole in the wall so that pilgrims could put their hands inside. They took out some of the dust, which they then put into water to give to the sick to drink; this was believed to restore them to health.

✠ Chronicle ✠

BORN
c.620 in Northumbria, England

DIED
Of natural causes following a brief illness, possibly the plague, on 2 March, 672 at Lichfield, England. It is thought his relics are now resting at Lichfield

PATRONAGE
Archdiocese of Birmingham, England; diocese of Lichfield, England

PRAYER ON ST CHAD'S FEAST DAY
Almighty God, whose servant Chad, for the peace of the Church, relinquished cheerfully the honours that had been thrust upon him, only to be rewarded with equal responsibility: Keep us, we pray, from thinking of ourselves more highly than we ought to think, and ready at all times to step aside for others (in honour preferring one another), that the cause of Christ may be advanced; in the name of him who washed his disciples' feet . . .

Joseph of Arimathea

Joseph of Arimathea was a wealthy upper-class Jew who was a member of the Sanhedrin in Jerusalem; he was also a secret follower of Jesus. After the crucifixion of Jesus, Joseph cast aside the secrecy and boldly asked Pontius Pilate for the body. This was a very courageous thing to do, as he was declaring his support for a condemned and executed criminal, but he took the risk in order to give Jesus an appropriate burial. The Gospel of Peter says that Joseph was a friend of Pilate, and that the burial of Jesus was negotiated before the crucifixion. Nightfall was approaching, and with it the Sabbath, so if Jesus's body remained on the cross it would have to be left there for another 24 hours. According to Jewish law, it was not permissible for the body of a criminal to be left hanging on a tree all night. Decency and Jewish law demanded that the body should be taken down.

With the help of Nicodemus the body of Jesus was taken down from the cross and laid in Joseph's own tomb in a nearby garden. Nicodemus supplied the spices, and Joseph the linen shroud. Joseph may have used his own tomb because it was close to the place of execution and the body needed to be buried quickly. Some have argued that Joseph was attempting to save Jesus's life, by getting him down early and reviving him in the privacy of his tomb. Pilate was surprised to hear that Jesus was dead, implying that death by crucifixion usually took longer.

All of this we are told in the Gospels, but at this point Joseph vanishes from the account. Nothing more is known about him. There is a medieval story that Joseph was sent by St Philip from Gaul to Britain in AD 63. He arrived at Glastonbury in a boat with eleven disciples. On landing he planted his staff, which instantly took root and became a tree, flowering every year at Christmas.

Joseph of Arimathea had a brief but important role to play in the story of Jesus. Much of the story is told from the point of view of the Galilean disciples of Jesus, and it is likely that the Gospels were written from their reminiscences, but when the narrative reaches its climax in Jerusalem there are hints that Jesus had a separate band of disciples in the city, with whom he was also in contact. Joseph of Arimathea was in all likelihood a leading figure among the Jerusalem disciples.

St Patrick

Chronicle

BORN

373 at Dumbarton in Scotland as Maewyn Succat

DIED

461–464 at Saul, County Down, Ireland

PATRONAGE

Baptismal font, demons, harp, snakes, snakes, cross, purgatory, serpent, shamrock

REPRESENTATION

Bishop driving snakes before him, bishop trampling on snakes

PRAYER

God our Father, you sent Saint Patrick to preach your glory to the people of Ireland. By the help of his prayers, may all Christians proclaim your love to all men. Grant this through our Lord Jesus Christ, your Son, who lives and reigns with you and the Holy Spirit, one God, for ever and ever.

St Patrick is Ireland's patron saint, yet little is known about him for certain. He was born at Dumbarton in Scotland in 373. His father was a deacon and a town councillor under the Roman administration. When he was fifteen, Patrick was captured by Irish raiders and for several years kept as a slave in Armagh in the north of Ireland. During that time, Patrick underwent a spiritual conversion. After seven years, he escaped back to Scotland, where he had dreams that seemed to tell him to return to Ireland as a missionary.

Patrick perhaps studied in Gaul and Italy before taking holy orders. After a long interval, when he was over sixty, he returned as a bishop and began his mission in Ireland. He decided to celebrate Easter on the Hill of Tara, at that time a centre of pagan worship. This was the scene of a set-piece confrontation between Patrick and the pagan 'wizards', a contest in which Patrick triumphed. In the wake of this, the saint composed a hymn called *The Deer's Cry*, then toured Ireland preaching and building churches.

Patrick was a bold and controversial figure. He was described as 'a lion in boldness, a serpent in cunning, a dove in gentleness and meekness.' He hoped to end his days in Armagh, but an angel warned him that this would not happen. Patrick lived to a great age and died at Saul in County Down. His funeral was a spectacular event, marked by all kinds of miracles, including the attendance of hosts of angels.

St Edward
King and Martyr

FEAST DAY: 18 MARCH

Edward the Martyr was born in 962 and was brought up by Sideman, Bishop of Crediton. When he was twelve or thirteen, in 975, he succeeded his father as King of the English, chosen by the witan under Dunstan's influence.

The young king was not to reign long. He was visiting his step-brother Ethelred, at Corfe Castle in Dorset in 978, when he met his end. One evening he approached the castle gate on horseback, and was met by members of his stepmother's household who gave him a cup of wine. This was merely a device to distract him. While he drank the wine he was cold-bloodedly stabbed in the back. He tried to turn his horse and ride away, but he soon lost consciousness and fell to the ground, dead.

Edward's body was unceremoniously buried in a marsh, but later reburied in the church at Wareham. Then it was exhumed and reburied once more with great pomp at Shaftesbury. Dunstan presided over the dead king's funeral. Afterwards, many miracles were reported at Edward's tomb.

The grounds for canonizing Edward may have been political. The step-brother for whom the murder was committed needed to show remorse for the assassination, and demanding canonization would have been a good way of demonstrating his contrition. There was also a surge of popular feeling, reflecting the personal qualities of the dead king that were considered admirable – gentleness, generosity, concern for the poor and needy. The official chronicler even broke into stilted verse:

> *There has not been among Angles*
> *A worse deed done*
> *Than this was.*

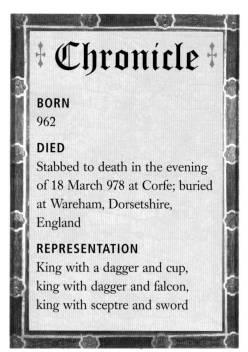

✝ Chronicle ✝

BORN
962

DIED
Stabbed to death in the evening of 18 March 978 at Corfe; buried at Wareham, Dorsetshire, England

REPRESENTATION
King with a dagger and cup, king with dagger and falcon, king with sceptre and sword

St Cuthbert

Cuthbert was born in 635 of poor parents, probably in Lauderdale in the Scottish Borders, and in what was then the kingdom of Northumbria. He was in many ways a very ordinary boy; he loved games, laughter and noise. His life changed one night in 651, while he was looking after sheep on the banks of the River Lauder. He had a vision of the soul of St Aidan rising to Heaven and the next day he decided he must become a monk.

He went straight to Melrose Abbey and presented himself to Prior Boisil, who could see that there was something unusual about the boy; 'Behold, an Israelite in whom there is no guile.' Cuthbert was exemplary, observing all of the abbey's strict rules. A few years later Abbot Eata was given land at Ripon by King Alcfrith of Northumbria. On this land a monastery was built, and Eata took Cuthbert to found it with the first group of monks.

Eata and Cuthbert suffered a setback in 661. Eata and his brothers refused to give up their British church services for Roman services, and for this they were expelled from Ripon. They went back to Melrose and when Boisil died Cuthbert became Prior at Melrose. Cuthbert frequently left Melrose, travelling to out-of-the-way places in the hills to preach; often he was away from the Abbey for weeks at a time, teaching the country people who would otherwise have no contact with the Church.

Cuthbert was appointed Prior of Lindisfarne, where he had the responsibility of introducing the Roman service, which he seems by this time to have been forced to accept. In 676, Cuthbert obtained permission from his abbot to retreat to the Farne Islands so that he could have greater solitude. There, two miles from Bamburgh, he built a cell and an oratory, surrounding them with a high wall so that he could see nothing but the sky. He received visitors there, but only to discuss their spiritual welfare.

In 684, at the Council of Twyford in Northumberland, King Egfrith of Northumbria pressed Cuthbert to become Bishop of Hexham. He accepted this office with great reluctance, and only after King Egfrith and Bishop Trumwine had personally persuaded him. Cuthbert was bishop for only two uneventful years, but his episcopate was exemplary. Just after Christmas in 686, he was boarding his boat to return to his cell on the Farne Islands when one of the monks standing on the shore asked him when they might hope for his return. Cuthbert replied, 'When you bring my body back.' He knew he was soon to die.

Two months later, Cuthbert fell ill and wanted to be left alone. His monks reluctantly went away as he asked, but were prevented from returning to the island by bad weather. When they did return after five days, Cuthbert was in a poor state, evidently dying, but was able to give his instructions as to his place of burial before he died, on 20 March 687.

Cuthbert's posthumous career was even more remarkable than his life and he was to become far more famous in death than in life. His body was treated to a special honour when it was reburied by his brethren on Lindisfarne Island in 689 in a lead-lined coffin. The famous illuminated Lindisfarne Gospels, among the greatest artwork of the millennium, were created to mark the occasion. Few people have been accorded an honour such as this.

Cuthbert's body was believed to be incorrupt. In 875, after the Viking raids began, the monks of Lindisfarne took Cuthbert's lead-lined coffin with them when they moved inland. After many wanderings, it found a resting-place at Chester-le-Street in 883. In 995 it was transferred to Ripon. The much-travelled body was finally buried in Durham Cathedral in 999.

There Cuthbert remained undisturbed, enclosed in an expensive and elaborate shrine and working his miracles on a daily basis, until the Reformation. His grave was opened in 1826. Inside a triple coffin, Cuthbert's skeleton was found, still intact, and dressed in robes of fine embroidered silk. Cuthbert's modern shrine is a simple, more fitting, symbolic creation.

Cuthbert held a unique place in English religious and social history as the most loved and honoured saint of northern England; churches were dedicated to him across a huge area, from the Rivers Trent and Mersey in the south to the Forth and the Clyde in the north.

St Benedict

Chronicle

BORN
480, Narsia, Umbria, Italy

DIED
Died of a fever on 21 March, 547 during prayer at Monte Cassino, Italy. He was buried with his sister in the same tomb at Monte Cassino

READING
With jubilation of the voice, O chant ye of our Father Benedict: The mouth of the righteous shall meditate wisdom. For wisdom hath built up a throne for herself in the bosom of the righteous man. And his tongue shall speak of judgement, seeing the Logos-teaching Pneumatos bedeweth the hidden places of his heart; for the law of his God is in his heart.

Born into a noble Roman family in AD 480, Benedict turned his back on the world at the age of fourteen, going off to live as a hermit in the mountains fifty miles from Rome. He lived alone in a cave for three years, after which he was persuaded to lead the monks of a neighbouring monastery. But his rule was strict, and one of the monks tried to poison him. Benedict withdrew to his cave.

Many monks visited him wanting to follow his way of life. He founded twelve small monasteries to accommodate them, with twelve monks in each monastery. But once again there were attempts on both his life and his virtue, and this time he withdrew to Monte Cassino. He was by now fifty years old, and at Monte Cassino he founded the Benedictine order.

The Benedictine order was to become the model for monastic life in Europe for 600 years. Other monastic orders were founded later – such as the Dominican and Franciscan – but they all grew out of the Benedictine order. The governing principle was separation from the everyday world. The world had to be renounced, silence had to be observed, therefore places far removed from the cities were chosen.

Benedict lived on at Monte Cassino for 14 years, becoming more and more celebrated. He died in 547, standing in front of the altar. In paintings Benedict is often depicted with his finger on his lip, telling us to be silent. The first words of his rule were, 'Give ear, my son.'

St Richard
of Chichester

Richard de Wych was born at Droitwich in Worcestershire in about 1197. He was the second son of wealthy parents. When his father died, Richard stayed at home to manage the family's chaotic financial affairs and it took several years of work to re-establish the family fortunes.

Then Richard went to Oxford to prepare for ordination. He was extremely poor while at Oxford, as the priest who was looking after his money stole it. He and two other students owned only one warm tunic and one gown between them, so they took it in turns to attend lectures.

Richard left Oxford to study canon law at Bologna. When he returned to England in 1235, he was made Chancellor of Canterbury by Archbishop Edmund Rich. Richard became Rich's devoted disciple, even following him into exile and remaining with him until he died in 1242.

After that, Richard lived in a Dominican monastery at Orléans and prepared to join the order, but was recalled by the new Archbishop of Canterbury to resume his Chancellorship. He also became Vicar of Deal in Kent. In 1244, he was elected Bishop of Chichester to replace Richard Passelew, King Henry III's choice, who had been dismissed by the Archbishop of Canterbury on grounds of incompetence. But the King refused to accept this, and for two years Richard was a homeless wanderer in his own diocese, unable to occupy the bishop's palace at Chichester. His temporary base during this unsatisfactory episode was the home of Simon, the Vicar of Tarring, which is now part of Worthing. At Simon's house, where he had to find useful ways of occupying his time, Richard became

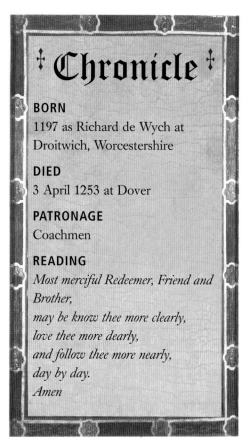

✠ Chronicle ✠

BORN
1197 as Richard de Wych at Droitwich, Worcestershire

DIED
3 April 1253 at Dover

PATRONAGE
Coachmen

READING
Most merciful Redeemer, Friend and Brother,
may be know thee more clearly,
love thee more dearly,
and follow thee more nearly,
day by day.
Amen

expert at tree-pruning and grafting. He also spent time fishing; he fished from the bridge over the tidal River Ouse at Lewes.

Once installed in his palace at Chichester, from 1246, Richard loved offering hospitality on a grand scale, and enjoyed good conversation. He used to write down anything he heard that he thought was interesting. His biographer, Ralph Bocking, was delighted when Richard said to him, 'The words which you said yesterday I have this night written down with my own hand.'

Richard was a vegetarian, out of consideration for the rights of animals. When lamb or chicken were served up at his table, he would address the dishes on the table in the following terms. 'If you were rational and could speak, how you would curse our gluttony! We have caused your death and, you innocents, what have you done to deserve it?'

In politics he opposed absolute monarchism. In his last year he preached a crusade. This began in Chichester Cathedral, and continued through the villages and towns of Sussex and Kent. He was summoned to preach the same cause in Westminster Abbey. His last formal act was to consecrate a church in Dover to the memory of his friend St Edmund of Canterbury. He died at Dover in April 1253 and was buried in his own cathedral, near the altar of St Edmund. It was believed that miracles took place at Richard's tomb, which led to his canonization in 1262.

Image supplied by kind permission of the Dean and Chapter, Chichester Cathedral

St Bernadette
of Lourdes

Bernadette was the eldest of the six children of François Soubirous, a poor miller. In 1858, when she was 14, Bernadette experienced a sequence of eighteen visions of the Virgin Mary at the rock of Massabielle at Lourdes. The visions all took place within the space of six extraordinary months, before and after which Bernadette's life was perfectly normal.

Bernadette's visions, which came to her when she was in one of her trances, were extremely simple in nature. Mary appeared and spoke to Bernadette about the need for prayer and penance. In the visions, Mary described herself as the Immaculate Conception, ordered the building of a church and told Bernadette to drink from a spring. From that moment on, the spring produced a huge volume of water.

Bernadette was a small, sickly girl who suffered from asthma. She was considered simple-minded, but her evident truthfulness, disinterestedness and courage were undisputed. She was interrogated strenuously by both public officials and clergy as they tried to expose what they assumed must be a hoax, but Bernadette was unswerving in her story.

She suffered a good deal from the unwanted publicity and the prurient curiosity about her. In 1866 she joined the Sisters of Notre Dame of Nevers, where she stayed for the rest of her life. She died at the early age of 35 after a long illness, which she bore with fortitude.

Remarkably, she stood back completely as Lourdes developed into a centre for pilgrimage – it was to become the biggest pilgrimage centre in modern times – and she even stayed away from the culminating moment of that development, the consecration of the basilica that Mary had asked for. Bernadette shied away from celebrity, amused that people wanted to buy photographs of her. She did not want to make her life extraordinary.

By the time Bernadette died in 1879 she was generally recognised by Catholics as a saint. The process of canonization was slow and cautious in the nineteenth century, and she was not formally called a saint until 1933. The Catholic Church recognised the sanctity of Bernadette, not so much because of her visions, but more for her total simplicity, commitment, self-denial and integrity. In these respects, Bernadette still stands alone among the modern visionaries.

St Alphege

Alphege was born of an aristocratic family in 953 or 954. While still a boy he adopted an ascetic life, against the wishes of his mother. He went to the monastery of Deerhurst in Gloucestershire before going off into an uninhabited area near Bath Abbey to build himself a hermit's cell. His reputation as a holy man grew and he was asked to take on the direction of Bath Abbey. He found the behaviour of the monks there lax, and imposed a tight and unrelenting discipline on them.

In 984, Alphege was consecrated as Bishop of Winchester, though he was still only 30. In this high profile position, Alphege's qualities became even more apparent. The ascetic regime continued, but he was not just a self-denying ascetic. He organized charitable work so effectively that there were no beggars in his diocese.

In 1006, when he was 52, Alphege became Archbishop of Canterbury. Then came his greatest trial. The Vikings were ravaging England, burning towns, farms and monasteries and massacring the inhabitants. Eventually Sweyn surrounded Canterbury. The English nobles pleaded with Alphege to get out while he could, but he chose to stay, saying that only a hireling would abandon his flock when danger threatened. Alphege tried to negotiate with the Vikings to spare the lives of innocent people, and encouraged the citizens to hold to their faith. The Vikings surged into Canterbury, slaughtering anyone who got in their way. The monks hoped to keep the Archbishop in the cathedral, where he might have been safe, but he confronted the Vikings.

'Spare these innocent people. There is no glory in spilling their blood. Turn your anger against me instead; I have

Chronicle

BORN
c.953

DIED
10 April, 1012

CANONIZED
1078

PRAYER
O loving God, whose martyr bishop Alphege of Canterbury suffered violent death because he refused to permit a ransom to be extorted from his people: Grant, we pray thee, that all pastors of thy flock may pattern themselves on the Good Shepherd, who laid down his life for the sheep; through him who with thee and the Holy Spirit liveth and reigneth, one God, for ever and ever. Amen.

reproached you for your cruelty.' The Vikings seized him and first made him watch as they burned down his cathedral and murdered his monks and citizens. Then they beat him and threw him into a dungeon where he was kept for some months.

The Vikings were stricken with a plague, which ceased when Alphege interceded with prayers. His captors were inclined to let him go then, but only if a substantial ransom was paid, three thousand marks in gold. On Easter Day, 10 April 1012, the 59-year-old Archbishop Alphege was paraded in front of the commander of the Viking fleet at Greenwich. He was threatened with torture and death if he did not produce the ransom. He replied that he could only offer them the gold of true wisdom, the knowledge and worship of the living God. He predicted that their empire in England would not last long.

They set upon him, beating him with the backs of their battle-axes and stoning him. One of the Vikings felt pity at Alphege's suffering and dealt him a death-blow with the sharp edge of his axe, splitting his skull.

Alphege's body was first taken for burial to St Paul's in London, and then later to his own cathedral at Canterbury. King Canute himself followed the body down the street to the waterfront, and held the stern of the boat as the martyr's body was laid in it.

St Anselm

Image by kind permission of the Chapter of Chester Cathedral

Born at Aosta in Italy in 1033, Anselm was for a time prevented from entering the Church by his wealthy father. Eventually he was allowed to travel to the Abbey of Bec in Normandy to be taught by Lanfranc; he became a monk. Anselm learned fast, and became Lanfranc's successor as prior after only three years, then abbot fifteen years later. He was to remain attached to the Abbey of Bec for many decades, and under him it became famous as a seat of learning.

Anselm was a great scholar, the greatest thinker ever to become Archbishop of Canterbury, but he also possessed great powers of sympathy, and these made him a powerful and effective teacher. All kinds of people visited him at Bec for advice, some of them extremely powerful. Even William the Conqueror, a notoriously brutal and unholy man, became mild and gentle in Anselm's presence. The Conqueror respected Anselm enormously; it was Anselm he asked for when he lay dying.

Anselm became a major figure at the English court. When William II lay ill, it was Anselm who was brought to his bedside. William had kept the archbishopric of

Canterbury vacant for three years in order to cream off the Canterbury revenues for himself, but as he lay ill in bed he pointed to Anselm as his chosen candidate. Anselm was very unwilling, but forced by the king to accept the appointment.

His reluctance was understandable. From then on his life was full of conflict, first with William, then with his successor, Henry I. He had to struggle against both of them to maintain the independence of the Church in England. Anselm was outspoken in his condemnation of what he saw as William II's immoral behaviour. He asked permission to hold a council of bishops to deal with a particularly gross sin of which the king himself was said to be guilty. The king refused, asking what they had planned to discuss. Anselm replied pointedly, 'The sin of Sodom and other detestable vices.'

Eventually, Anselm decided to withdraw to Rome for advice and protection. He was there when the king was assassinated while out hunting, but his relationship with William's successor, and probable murderer, Henry I, was no better.

Anselm's public life was full of frustrations, but behind the scenes he was conducting highly productive correspondence with a large network of powerful men, including the King of the Scots, the Irish High King and the King of Jerusalem, all of whom sought his wise advice. He also wrote several scholarly works characterised by a lack of dogma, including a treatise on free will. On Palm Sunday 1109 Anselm fell ill and died a few days later, on 21 April, at the age of 75. He was buried in Canterbury Cathedral – in front of the rood screen next to Lanfranc – but later his remains were moved to the chapel which still bears his name. It was Thomas Becket who requested Anselm's canonization in 1163.

Anselm's life represents one episode in the continuing struggle for supremacy between Church and state in medieval Europe, a bitter struggle that was to continue for hundreds of years.

☩ Chronicle ☩

BORN
1033 at Aosta, Piedmont, Italy

DIED
Anselm died at Canterbury, England on 21 April, 1109 and it is believed that his body is buried in the churchyard at Canterbury Cathedral

REPRESENTATION
Benedictine monk admonishing an evildoer or as an archbishop

PRAYER
O Lord, we bring before you the distress and dangers of peoples and nations, the pleas of the imprisoned and the captive, the sorrows of the grief-stricken, the needs of the refugee, the impotence of the weak, the weariness of the despondent, and the diminishments of the aging. O Lord, stay close to all of them. Amen

St George

George was born at Lydda in Palestine of parents who came from Cappadocia, now part of Turkey. His father, a rich imperial officer, died when George was ten. George himself became a soldier at seventeen, rising to the rank of tribune in the reign of the Emperor Diocletian.

St George was known for his outstanding good looks, courtesy and courage. When Diocletian launched his persecution of the Christians, George was indignant at the injustice of it. He retired from the army and tried to plead the cause of the Christians before the emperor. First he returned to Lydda, freed his slaves and gave away his money, then he set off to meet the Emperor, fully expecting that the result would be his own execution. It was while on this journey that he is supposed, according to one version of his life only, to have encountered the famous dragon at Beirut.

In the *Golden Legend*, the dragon terrorised the people who lived near it, consuming both sheep and children below the age of fifteen, who were offered to the dragon in a kind of lottery. The lot finally fell to the king's daughter, and it was at the moment when she was being led towards the dragon's lair that St George happened to be passing through on horseback. St George stopped to ask why she was in tears. She explained and he told her he would save her. He miraculously killed the dragon, which prompted the king and all his people to agree to be baptised.

St George then went to the imperial court at Nicomedia to appeal on behalf of the Christians, with the inevitable result. He was imprisoned and tortured with a huge stone laid on his chest, but he steadfastly refused to give up Christianity. The temple priests denounced George as a magician and demanded that Diocletian order his execution. George was beheaded on 28 April 303. His body was taken to Lydda, where the Emperor Constantine later raised a church over his tomb.

In rescuing a damsel in distress, St George epitomised the important medieval ideal of chivalry. In standing up fearlessly for what he knew to be right, knowingly risking death in making himself the champion of a cause, he was also the great role model for young men in the middle ages. When the Crusaders returned to England they brought their loyalty to St George with them, and in this roundabout way he became the patron saint of England. He is invariably shown as a medieval knight in the act of slaying the dragon, which became a potent symbol of paganism.

St Mark

✠ Chronicle ✠

BORN
Not documented

DIED
St Mark was martyred at Alexandria on 25 April, 68. His relics lie in a basilica in Venice, Italy

PATRONAGE
Against impenitence, attorneys, barristers, captives, Egypt, glaziers, imprisoned people, prelature of Infanta, Philippines, insect bites, lawyers, lions, notaries, prisoners, scrofulous diseases, stained glass workers, struma, diocese of Venice

REPRESENTATION
St Mark is often represented with a lion in the desert or as a bishop on a throne which is decorated with lions. He can also be seen as a man writing his gospel, or rescuing Christian slaves from Saracens

Mark was the cousin of Barnabas and son of Mary whose house was a meeting place of the disciples of Jesus at Jerusalem. He is thought to be the young man who ran away naked from the Garden of Gethsemane when Jesus was arrested.

Mark went with Paul and Barnabas on their first missionary journey, though he left them at Perga and went back to Jerusalem. Perhaps he disapproved of Paul's practice of preaching to Gentiles; perhaps he returned home because he lost his nerve. Three or four years later, Barnabas proposed taking Mark on the next missionary journey, but Paul refused and there was a sharp disagreement between them resulting in their separation. Paul went to Syria with Silas, and Barnabas sailed to Cyprus with Mark.

After another ten years, when Paul was in Rome, the rift had healed and Paul spoke of Mark as a fellow worker. Peter too regarded Mark as a valuable fellow worker, referring to him as 'my son'. It is believed that Mark went to Rome with Peter and acted as his interpreter. He wrote the Gospel according to St Mark in Rome and is said to have been helped in this task by Peter.

After the death of St Peter in Rome, Mark is said to have preached in Alexandria. Eventually he was set upon and dragged through the streets by a mob shouting, 'Let us drag the wild ox to the slaughter house!' He died of his injuries.

St James the Less

FEAST DAY: 1 MAY

✠ Chronicle ✠

BORN
Not known

DIED
In 62AD James was condemned to death by stoning and finally clubbed to death while praying for his attackers

PATRONAGE
Apothecaries, druggists, dying people, fullers, hatmakers, hatters, milliners and pharmacists

PRAYER
O Glorious Saint James, you were our Lord's cousin and at the same time his friend and follower. You wrote that every good and perfect gift comes to us from the Father of lights, and that faith without works is useless. You preached the divinity of Jesus until your death as a martyr . . .

James is believed to have been the younger brother of Jesus by those who believe that Mary was a virgin at the time of Jesus's birth, though not afterwards. Those who believe that Mary remained a virgin all her life, suppose that Joseph was married before he was betrothed to Mary and that James was the son of this earlier marriage.

James seems not to have believed that his brother was the Messiah until after the Resurrection. St Paul said that Jesus made a posthumous appearance to James on his own. After that, James took the leading role in the Church of Jerusalem. He was later regarded as the first Bishop of Jerusalem, but it is unlikely that he ever thought of himself in those terms. James acted as President of the Council which decided the extent to which Gentiles had to conform to Jewish customs when becoming Christians.

James was nicknamed James the Just, and it was said that his knees were as hard as a camel's through his constant kneeling in prayer in the Temple. He was the author of the Epistle of St James.

James was condemned to be stoned by the Sanhedrin. While lying half-dead, he was killed with a fuller's club. The siege of Jerusalem, which followed, was seen by many in Jerusalem – even the non-Christians – as a divine judgement for the crime of assassinating James.

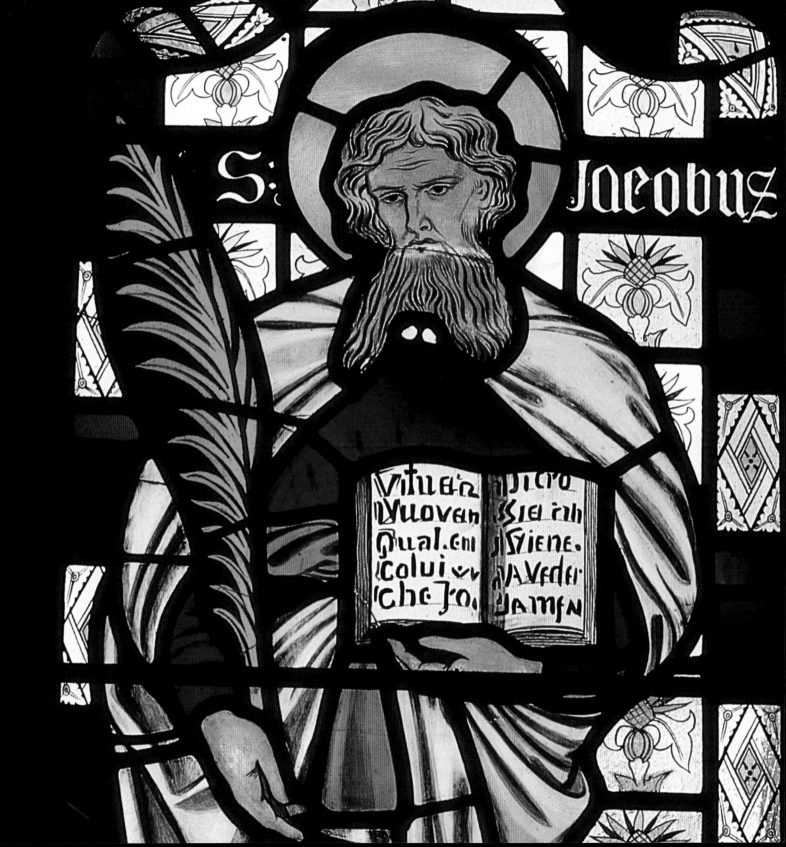

St Brendan

the Navigator

Chronicle

BORN

c.495 Kerry, Ireland

DIED

He died c.577 at Enachduin (now Annaghdown) and was interred in Clonfert, Ireland

PATRONAGE

Boatmen, mariners, sailors, travellers, watermen, whales

PRAYER

God of sea and land, you endowed your servant Brendan with a bold and adventurous spirit, to occupy himself for your business on the great waters, and revealed to him your wonders in the deep . . .

Brendan the Navigator was an Irish saint of whom wonderful tales were told. Brendan, not to be confused with his contemporary, Brendan of Birr, was born around AD 495. Among the many stories about him, the most outstanding were about his voyages. Brendan sailed the ocean for seven years, seeing all kinds of wonders, including whales and unknown islands, before returning home. On a second voyage, Brendan sailed west to find the Land of Promise. Eventually he found an island carpeted with flowers and steeped in heavenly music.

Pre-Christian beliefs about the souls of the dead travelling to a mystic island far to the west, and possibly a genuine Atlantic voyage of discovery, have been added to the life of a Christian saint. Brendan was allegedly a contemporary of King Arthur. Geoffrey of Monmouth mentions a man called Barinthus in his *Life of Merlin*, and makes him an otherworldly ferryman, a Celtic Charon, who guides both Merlin and Taliesin to Avalon with the wounded Arthur. Barinthus, 'the Navigator', acquired a reputation in bardic literature as an accomplished sailor who could navigate by the stars. The story of the Brendan voyages also features Barinthus as St Barrind; he was Brendan's captain. In legend, it is said that Arthur may have commissioned an Irish flotilla to rescue him from the Mawddach estuary after his disastrous defeat at Camlan.

St Dunstan

✠ Chronicle ✠

BORN
909 at Baltonsborough, Glastonbury, England

DIED
He died of natural causes in 988 at Canterbury, England. He was buried at Canterbury where his tomb became a popular place for pilgrims to visit during the Middle Ages

PATRONAGE
Armourers, blacksmiths, blind people, gold workers, goldsmiths, jewellers, lighthouse keepers, locksmiths, musicians, silver workers, silversmiths, swordsmiths

REPRESENTATION
In the stained glass picture (*right*) St Dunstan is depicted holding a staff and a pair of pincers. He has also been represented with a troop of angels and a dove hovering close by

Dunstan was a West Saxon aristocrat; his family's estates were near Glastonbury and it was natural that as a boy he should be sent to Glastonbury Abbey to be educated. He spent part of his youth at the court of King Athelstan, where he experienced dreams and visions that he believed were supernatural. He was a thoughtful, studious boy but he was unpopular with his companions, who complained to the King that Dunstan was practising magic. Athelstan agreed to his banishment from court, and the boys threw him into a marsh.

Dunstan went next to his kinsman Alphege, then Bishop of Winchester. Alphege tried to persuade Dunstan to become a monk, but Dunstan resisted on the grounds that he might want to get married. Then Dunstan became seriously ill, which altered his perspective. Subsequently he took vows and went to Glastonbury Abbey.

There, Dunstan lived in a tiny cell where he spent much of his time in thought and prayer. He also developed considerable skills as a painter, embroiderer and metalworker. He had more visions. When Athelstan died and Edmund became king, Dunstan was recalled to court, though he was soon driven out again. The new king narrowly escaped death in a hunting accident near Cheddar, attributing his survival to a miracle of prayer. Edmund recalled Dunstan and asked him to ride with him to Glastonbury, where they knelt together in prayer and then the king installed the 21-year-old Dunstan in the abbot's seat.

Edmund 'The Magnificent' was assassinated shortly afterwards and buried at Glastonbury. His successor and brother Edred was also on friendly terms with Dunstan, offering him the bishopric of Crediton, which he declined. Edred died in 955, to be succeeded by the 16-year-old Edwy, the son of Edmund, who instantly quarrelled with Dunstan. Edwy disappeared from the coronation banquet in order to have sex with two women, a mother and daughter, and it was Dunstan who was given the unenviable task of fetching him. Dunstan's biographer describes 'the crown thrown carelessly on the floor' and the teenage king with the women 'repeatedly wallowing between the two of them in evil fashion, as if in a vile sty.' Dunstan forcibly removed Edwy. Edwy married the younger of the two women, Aelgifu; inevitably Dunstan was exiled for having interfered.

Dunstan stayed at a monastery in Ghent, where he was able to observe the Benedictine rule in action. Two years later, Edgar became king, and Dunstan was made first Bishop of Worcester then Bishop of London. In 961 he became Archbishop of Canterbury. Dunstan remained Edgar's wise adviser until Edgar's death in 975, and it was to a great extent due to Dunstan that Edgar became the first king of the whole of England. He was certainly a man of sufficient stature. He loved to mend quarrels and to befriend the poor and needy. He was a loving and gentle man, easily moved to tears. He was also an untiring teacher and is said to have filled all England with his light.

St Augustine
of Canterbury

Augustine was prior of a monastery in Rome when Pope Gregory the Great commissioned him to convert the English. He set off with a band of forty monks and along the way they heard frightening stories about the savages they would meet across the Channel. They sent Augustine back to try to persuade Gregory to change his mind, but it was to no avail.

In 597, after dawdling across Gaul, they landed on the Isle of Thanet off the Kent coast, no doubt filled with apprehension. King Ethelbert of Kent had married a Frankish princess, Bertha. A Christian with her own chaplain, she used the ancient and half-ruined church of St Martin in Canterbury. King Ethelbert himself was suspicious of the new religion, especially as presented by Augustine's monks with their silver crosses, banners and strange litany, but he let the missionaries use St Martin's as their base. This modest-looking but incredibly ancient little church still stands.

Augustine's reception was not as hostile as he had expected, and the persuasive Bertha evidently worked towards converting the king. After a time, Ethelbert was baptised, and inevitably many subjects rushed to follow the king's example. The next Christmas ten thousand converts were baptised in the Medway estuary. Augustine was consecrated 'Bishop of the English' and set up a monastery on the site of the old Roman basilica; this structure eventually became Canterbury Cathedral.

In 601 Gregory sent Augustine his plan for the organisation of the English Church, which was to have two archbishops, one at London and one at York. Shortly after this, Augustine held a conference at Aust by the Severn crossing into Wales with priests of the ancient British Church.

It was possibly on this journey west that Augustine encountered committed pagans at Cerne Abbas, where he was sent packing after challenging the locals. It seems the Cerne Giant and the spring nearby were a focus for pagan worship. Gregory advised Augustine not to destroy such pagan sanctuaries, but to turn them into Christian sanctuaries. This is probably why Cerne Abbey was built between the Cerne Giant and the spring called 'St Augustine's Well'.

In 604, Augustine appointed Mellitus as Bishop of the East Saxons, with his seat in London, and Justus as Bishop of Rochester. He died on 26 May that year.

St Philip Neri

✠ Chronicle ✠

BORN
22 July, 1515 at Florence, Italy

DIED
27 May, 1595

NAME MEANING
Lover of horses

BEATIFIED
11 May, 1615 by Pope Paul V

CANONIZED
12 March, 1622 by Pope Gregory XV

PATRONAGE
Rome, Italy, United States Army Special Forces

PRAYER
Cheerfulness strengthens the heart and makes us persevere in a good life. Therefore the servant of God ought always to be in good spirits.

Philip Neri was born in Florence in 1515, the son of a well-to-do notary, Francesco Neri. He was well educated, though he fell for a time under the influence of the Dominicans at San Marco, where the notorious Savonarola had been a friar within living memory. At the age of 18, Philip had a deep religious experience, left his uncle's business and went to Rome, where he lived as a layman for seven years, earning his living by teaching, and living virtually the life of a hermit. He also wrote poetry and studied theology and philosophy.

At that time, Rome was in a poor state morally, and Philip Neri began working with young men. He founded a lay brotherhood, which met for worship and to offer help to pilgrims, the sick and the convalescent. This initiative gradually became the Trinity Hospital. Philip spent a lot of time in prayer, especially at night and in the catacomb of St Sebastian. It was there, in 1544, that Philip Neri had an intense mystical experience in which he felt that a globe of fire entered him through the mouth and swelled his heart. He felt it as a pang of divine love, and it was so powerful that it left a permanent physical effect on his heart, as was discovered when his heart was examined after his death.

In 1551, Philip Neri was ordained priest, and went to live at the clergy house of San Girolamo, where he became a renowned confessor. But his main work was still with young men. Philip had an engaging and attractive personality and had no difficulty chatting to the young and persuading them to give up their immoral ways. An oratory was built above the church, where religious discussions were held as well as services consisting of musical compositions on religious themes; they were arranged for solo voices and choir. This gave rise to the name of a new form of art work, the oratorio.

By 1575, Philip had formed all these elements into the Congregation of the Oratory, in which the path to perfection was for lay people, just as much as for monks and nuns. The Oratorians became best known in England through the work of Cardinal Newman, who founded the Brompton Oratory and the London Oratory. St Philip built a new church for his Congregation, the Chiesa Nuova, and became a celebrated figure in Rome, where his uplifting spiritual influence was overwhelming. Some Romans were shocked by his unconventional speech and actions, but he carried on working towards his goal. St Philip was always happy and considerate, sometimes indulging in practical jokes. This lightness of heart did not prevent him from being seen as a saint even during his lifetime. St Philip Neri was a likeable man, humble, gentle, energetic, cheerful, friendly and full of good humour.

On 27 May 1595, at the end of a normal day of seeing visitors, Philip said, 'Last of all, we must die.' A few hours later he had a haemorrhage and died.

The Venerable Bede

Bede was born in 673 not far from Jarrow in Northumbria in north-east England. When he was seven years old he was sent to the Benedictine monastery at Wearmouth, to study under the care of Benedict Biscop. In 682 he moved to the new monastery at Jarrow. Bede later wrote, 'From that time, dwelling all my life in that monastery, I have given all my labour to the study of the Scriptures; and amid the observance of monastic discipline and the daily duty of chanting in the church I have ever delighted to learn or teach or write.'

When Bede was a boy, plague struck Jarrow and everyone at the monastery except himself and Abbot Ceolfrid died. He was conscientious about attending services. He once said to his fellow monks, 'I know that angels are present at the gatherings of the brethren. What if they do not find me among them? They will say, "Where is Bede?"'

Bede is one of the early saints about whom we know most, simply because he wrote freely about himself and what went on around him. At 19 he became a deacon and at 30, in 703, he was ordained a priest by Bishop John, 'at the bidding of Abbot Ceolfrid'. In terms of outward events, very little happened to Bede. His was a life of quiet prayer and uninterrupted scholarship. It seems he never travelled outside Northumbria.

Bede inspired love among his fellow monks, and one of them wrote a full and touching description of his last days as he lay dying at Easter in 735. 'By turns we read and by turns we wept. Nay, we wept always while we read.' Bede tried to carry on writing by dictation. One of his disciples reminded him that there was a chapter to finish. Bede said, 'Get out your pen and write quickly.' Another disciple wrote an epitaph and got as far as: *Hac sunt in fossa, Bedae - - - ossa.*

'Here in this tomb are the bones of - - - Bede.' The monk went to bed and the next morning found that an angel had filled in the gap with the word 'venerabilis'. The adjective stuck to Bede from that time forward; he is still invariably referred to as 'the Venerable Bede'.

He wrote copiously, leaving behind over 40 works. Among them is his *Ecclesiastical History of the English People*, which is the single most important source for early English history. Bede wrote it in Latin, but King Alfred caused it to be translated into Anglo-Saxon, or perhaps even translated it himself. Towards the end of his life, Bede translated St John's Gospel into Anglo-Saxon, an early step towards making the Bible more accessible to ordinary people. Bede was formally canonized in 1899.

St Joan of Arc

Joan of Arc was born at the village of Domrémy on the River Meuse, in 1412. Her parents were stock-owning peasants. France was overrun by English and Burgundian armies. The heir apparent to the French throne, the Dauphin; was powerless and could not even enter his own capital for his coronation. But it was not just the élite of France who were affected. The armies of occupation made food production difficult, and even the peasants suffered.

It was in this desperate context, a time of national crisis, that at the age of twelve or thirteen Joan started having visions and hearing voices. A voice from a cloud told her to go to the aid of the King of France. She must wear men's clothes, take up arms and lead the French soldiers. At other times, she heard the voices of St Catherine, St Margaret and St Michael, but she recognised Christ as her Master. The voices told her to see that the Dauphin was crowned at Rheims and to deliver France from her enemies.

At first Joan resisted her voices. Eventually, in 1428, she told the captain of the nearest town of her mission, but when she asked him to take her to the Dauphin he laughed at her. The next year she tried again. This time she was escorted to meet the Dauphin at Chinon. She was eventually accepted, given a household, a horse and armour. Then she joined the French troops in a suit of white armour and carrying a little battle-axe.

Joan took part in the attacks on Orléans, quickly assuming command. She had an instinct for military command and was often to be seen leading an assault. She was wounded several times. Victory followed victory until she achieved her goal – the coronation of the Dauphin as Charles V at Rheims. The war with Burgundy was not over, though. In May 1430 at Compiègne, she was attacked by Burgundians, captured and sold to the English. From the start, the English had sworn to burn Joan as a witch if they ever caught her.

Joan was kept under the harshest conditions in prison, and the ungrateful French King made no attempt to save her. Her trial for heresy was long and cruelly unjust. A recantation was drawn out of her in exchange for a promise of a lenient sentence, life-long penance in a convent, but still she was not released from prison, and she revoked her recantation. Then she was sentenced to be burnt to death.

On 30 March 1431, Joan was led out into the Old Market at Rouen. Her tormentors put on her head a paper mitre bearing the words, 'Heretic. Relapsed. Apostate.' An English soldier, taking pity on her, gave her a cross made of two sticks; she held it as she was chained to the stake. After they burnt her, they threw her ashes into the Seine.

St Boniface (Winfrith)

Boniface was born as Winfrith at Crediton in Devon in about 680. He was the son of Saxon settlers and would never forget his Germanic roots. As a boy he showed high intelligence and was sent to study at Nursling, near Southampton. He made rapid progress there and was soon appointed schoolmaster; he wrote a Latin grammar and a book on the scansion of poetry.

When he was thirty he was ordained as a priest. Early on he won the trust of King Ine of Wessex, who sent him on a diplomatic mission to Archbishop Bertwald of Canterbury. The scholastic life at Nursling suited Winfrith well, but although it was tempting to stay there, or seek some promotion within the English Church, he felt a nagging compulsion to become a missionary. Above all, he wanted to convert pagan Saxony (northern Germany) to Christianity.

In 718 he set off for Rome to meet Pope Gregory II, who knew nothing of Winfrith as yet, but agreed to commission him to travel to Germany to convert pagans. He made his way to Frisia, where he assisted Willibrord for two years. Willibrord wanted Winfrith to stay there and succeed him as bishop, but he refused on the grounds that he had promised the Pope he would convert Germany.

Word filtered back to Rome about Winfrith's huge successes – he had converted thousands of Frisians – and the Pope decided to make him bishop over all those who remained leaderless. Winfrith had a major success at Geismar (central Germany), where he destroyed the sacred tree of Thor. This was taken as a sign that his God was more powerful than Thor, and won him many converts.

Winfrith's life was an extremely complex one. He spent a great deal of time preaching and converting people. He also spent a great deal of time in diplomatic and political activity. In the 740s, he was able to reform the Frankish Church by developing close ties with the brothers Carloman and Pippin, joint rulers of the Kingdom of the Franks. In 751 Winfrith was responsible for devising and stage-managing the coronation of Pippin as King of the Franks. It was such a profoundly effective and impressive ritual that it was to be imitated by one king after another from that time on.

Correspondence was another of Winfrith's major activities. A surprising number of Winfrith's letters survive, and they show him as a subtle and sophisticated thinker who was able to find exactly the right things to say to his reader. He corresponded with priests, bishops, abbesses, popes and kings, and the all-inclusive range of his friends marks him out as one of the most influential figures of his age.

He made one final expedition north to Frisia, apparently with the idea of establishing Christianity on the western frontier of Saxony. In 754 he was encamped with some followers at Dokkum, when he was attacked, probably by brigands, and killed. This turned him instantly into a martyr, and his body was taken by way of Utrecht and Mainz back to the place that he had made his headquarters, the Abbey of Fulda.

St Boniface was a giant among early medieval saints; and as a result of his work in central and northern Europe, a great swathe of Europe became Christian from the North Sea to the Mediterranean. The Christian Church also developed into a more formal, uniform and unified institution. Winfrith was largely responsible for creating what we nowadays think of as the Roman Catholic Church, centrally controlled under papal authority. Oddly, the popes he worked with did not always appreciate his efforts on their behalf; he was at least once admonished for being too hard on his fellow priests. Winfrith had a vision for a strong, united Church, and did much to create it. He also had a vision of a unified Europe, where there would be but one people. He was, like St Paul, an internationalist on the grand scale.

St Columba of Iona

Columba was born in Donegal in Ireland on 7 December AD 521, the day St Buite, the founder of Monasterboice, died. He was a prince of the O'Donnell clan and was baptised at Temple Douglas.

Columba travelled to Strangford Lough, where he became a pupil of St Finnian and was ordained deacon. He went on south to Leinster to study under the aged bard, Gemman. In 544 an outbreak of plague caused him to return to the north. In 546, Columba founded the religious community at Derry. This was the first of a series of foundations; his most famous was Kells. His favourite occupation was copying manuscripts and he transcribed three hundred copies of the Gospels with his own hand.

A quarrel blew up with King Diarmid in 561 and a battle took place, the Battle of Cooldrevny, at Columba's instigation. Columba was condemned and excommunicated by a Church court convened at Teltown in Meath, though the synod was not unanimous: St Brendan was one of those who dissented. The excommunication was later withdrawn and he was sentenced to perpetual exile from Ireland. In 563, with twelve followers, Columba set sail at the age of 42. He landed first at Oronsay, but because Ireland was still in sight, he sailed on to Iona, then known as Hy.

Columba founded a religious community on Iona, with a chapel and beehive cells of wood and wattle. Columba used Iona as his base for the conversion of the still-pagan Picts living on the Scottish mainland. He became the personal 'soul-friend' or confessor to two kings and a saint, as well as to a host of ordinary people. Iona became an important religious focus, and Columba was visited by many of his fellow-monks from Ireland: St Finbar, St Comgall, St Brendan, St Ronan, St Flannan and many others came on visits to Columba's sacred island.

When his friend and admirer St Brendan of Birr, a frequent visitor to Iona, died in 573, Columba launched a festival in his memory. The following year King Conall of Dalriada died and Columba formally inaugurated his successor, Aidan, on Iona. From then on, for hundreds of years, Iona became a place of special royal sanctity and the burial place of many kings.

Columba, one of the greatest saints of the British Isles, died at Iona in 597. A long and detailed biography of Columba, full of picturesque visions, angels and demons, was written by Adamnan, the ninth Abbot of Iona.

St Barnabas

Chronicle

BORN

In Cyprus as Joseph

DIED

St Barnabas was martyred *c.*61 at Salamis, and it is thought that he was stoned to death. It has also been recorded that he was holding a copy of the Gospel of Saint Matthew which he had written out by hand

PATRONAGE

Against hailstorms, Antioch, Cyprus, invoked as peacemaker

MEMORIAL

11 June

ACTS 4:36f

Joseph, a Levite, born in Cyprus, whom the apostles called Barnabas (son of encouragement), sold a field he owned, brought the money, and turned it over to the apostles.

The name Barnabas means 'son of consolation'. He was originally a Cypriot called Joseph, and was given the name Barnabas by Jesus's other disciples. He joined them after he sold a field and laid the money at the feet of the apostles.

When St Paul arrived in Jerusalem after his conversion, the disciples were afraid of him; it was Barnabas who mediated. Barnabas was sent on a mission to Antioch, where some of the disciples were preaching to non-Jewish Greeks. Barnabas joined Paul at Tarsus, where the two men preached together. Their strategy of preaching to non-Jews – a significant new development – set them apart from the other disciples.

On their first joint missionary journey, they were accompanied by Barnabas's nephew. Barnabas was mistaken for Jupiter and Paul for Mercury, which gives an idea of the charismatic personalities of the two men. In the Gospel of St Luke, it is clear that Barnabas was regarded as a figure who was as important as Paul.

When the second missionary journey was being planned, Barnabas wanted to take his nephew Mark again, even though Mark had deserted them during the first journey. Paul would not hear of it, and the two men parted company. Barnabas went to Cyprus, Paul to Syria. After that, Barnabas is not mentioned again in the documents. It is believed that he met his end as a martyr at Salamis. It is odd that such a prominent and significant figure should disappear without trace.

St Alban

When St Germanus visited the town of Verulamium (now St Albans in England) in 429, he worshipped in a church containing the remains of a martyr named Alban. Germanus took away some soil from the spot as a keepsake and was keen to find out more. Not much was recorded about Alban, then or later. Alban was a Roman soldier stationed in Verulamium. Tradition has it that he died during the persecution of Christians in the reign of the Emperor Diocletian in 304, but it now seems more likely that he died in 209, during an earlier persecution under the Emperor Septimius Severus. Septimius Severus was married to Julia Domna, the daughter of a Syrian high priest of the pagan god Elagabal.

A priest fleeing for his life from the authorities came to Alban's house and Alban gave him shelter. As they conversed during the next few days, Alban became more and more impressed by the priest and his teachings. The Roman authorities eventually tracked the fugitive down to Alban's house. When they knocked at the door, Alban answered, wearing the priest's clothes.

When Alban was taken before the judges, who ordered him to renounce Christianity, he confirmed that he was a Christian and bound by Christian obligations. Then his true identity emerged. The judge pressed him to put aside Christianity and offer sacrifice to the pagan deities, but Alban refused. The judge condemned him to death.

On the way to the hill which was to be the place of execution, Alban and his executioners were held up by the great crowd that had gathered. To express their sympathy for Alban, they accompanied him out of the town towards the hill. The bridge over a stream was jammed with people. Alban decided to go to one side and cross the stream. As he approached, Alban prayed aloud and the stream dried up to let him pass. The executioner was so overwhelmed when he saw this that he threw down his sword, fell at Alban's feet and told him he could not behead him. When they arrived at the top of the hill, Alban prayed for water and a spring broke out under his feet. Another soldier was called forward to behead Alban. When he did so, his eyes are reported to have burst out of their sockets; he was blinded at the instant of Alban's death. Yet another soldier came forward to execute the converted executioner.

When the unfortunate priest heard that Alban had been arrested, he hurried to the court, intending to give himself up and so save Alban. By this time Alban was already dead, but the judge sentenced the priest to death, too.

Septimius Severus died two years later in York. The persecution of the Christians ceased and they were able to come out of their hiding places and once again worship openly. They built a small 'church of suitable dignity' on the site of the three executions on the hill. That church was eventually replaced with a larger building, St Alban's Abbey, by Offa King of Mercia in 793. The remains of Alban were destroyed at Henry VIII's orders, but his splendid shrine still stands in the abbey.

✠ Chronicle ✠

BORN
429 in Verulamium, Hertfordshire (now St Albans), England

DIED
Beheaded on Verulamium Hill, England and buried in an adjoining cemetery

PATRONAGE
Converts, refugees, torture victims

REPRESENTATION
St Alban is often represented in civil or military dress, bearing the palm of martyrdom and a sword, or, alternatively, a cross and a sword

PRAYER
Almighty God, by whose grace and power your holy martyr Alban triumphed over suffering and was faithful even unto death: Grant to us, who now remember him with thanksgiving, to be so faithful in our witness to you in this world, that we may receive with him the crown of life; through Jesus Christ our Lord, who lives and reigns with you and the Holy Spirit, one God, for ever and ever. Amen.

St Thomas More

Thomas More was born in London in 1478, the son of a judge, Sir John More. He was sent at the age of 13 to join the household of the Archbishop of Canterbury. Later, after studying under the renowned humanist scholar Thomas Linacre at Oxford, and then at Lincoln's Inn, he was called to the bar. In 1504 he became a Member of the English Parliament, though he was still debating, inwardly, what sort of life he really wanted to lead. He thought seriously about becoming a Carthusian monk or a friar, or a diocesan priest. Even after his marriage to Jane Colt he was still drawn to the monastic life, and wore a hair shirt. He was a man, like Thomas Becket, leading a double life.

More's political career developed rapidly, and his reputation for scholarly brilliance grew with the publication of his writings, especially *Utopia* in 1516. He was famously the friend of Erasmus. After holding a series of major posts, he was made Lord Chancellor after the fall of Wolsey in 1529, despite making it clear that he did not want the position. He disagreed with Henry VIII when the King tried to wield power over the Church. At first he accepted Henry's title 'Protector and Supreme Head of the Church in England', but as the division with Rome progressed he realised that he could not remain in office. He retired to Chelsea, refusing to attend the coronation of Anne Boleyn and refusing to sign the oath recognising the children of Henry and the new Queen Anne as heirs to the throne. He was now making it plain that he had not approved of the King's divorce from Katherine of Aragon.

Henry VIII would not tolerate this defiance and had More arrested and imprisoned in the Tower of London in 1534. More refused to comment on the Act of Supremacy in 1535, and at his trial his silence was interpreted as treasonable opposition. He was condemned to death for treason, and beheaded on 6 July 1535. On the scaffold, he claimed to be 'the King's good servant, but God's first.'

More was beatified in 1886 and canonized in 1935. He is one of the few English saints to be universally revered in the Catholic Church. Not only did he die as a martyr in the defence of the Church: his life as a whole was God-centred. He is often remembered as civilised and humane, saintly in the conventional sense. But Sir Thomas More was more complicated than that. There was another side to More. His condemnation of William Tyndale for translating the Bible into English was expressed in surprisingly vitriolic language. On one occasion he described Tyndale as 'a bag of pus'. He hated Tyndale with all his heart, and some have even suggested that More, though himself imprisoned in the Tower, organised the ambush in Belgium which led to Tyndale's death by burning, another martyr in another cause.

St John Fisher

John Fisher was born in Beverley in 1469. He was educated at Cambridge, where he became a Fellow of Michaelhouse. In 1501 he was appointed Vice-Chancellor of Cambridge University. Then the following year he dramatically resigned both chancellorship and fellowship to become Chaplain to Lady Margaret Beaumont, Henry VIII's mother.

Fisher and Lady Margaret worked together to reform and endow the university, founding two new colleges – St John's and Christ's. Fisher became Chancellor of Cambridge University in 1504, and Bishop of Rochester in the same year. His sermons were widely read throughout Europe, and those against Luther were especially acclaimed.

Fisher's troubles began when he became Katherine of Aragon's confessor. As Henry VIII moved relentlessly towards divorcing Katherine, Fisher implacably opposed him. It was Fisher who led the opposition to Henry's seizure of supremacy in the Church. He was only ready to accept Henry's new title 'head of the Church in England' with the addition of the clause, 'so far as the law of Christ allows.' Henry VIII was furious.

In 1534 Fisher was sent to the Tower of London, along with Sir Thomas More. Frantic attempts were made in the Vatican to save him – he was named a cardinal by the new Pope Paul III – but Henry was determined to destroy him. Fisher was condemned to death for high treason and beheaded in 1535, courteous to the last – even to his executioner.

Like More, Fisher was formally declared a saint in 1935; the two men share a midsummer feast day.

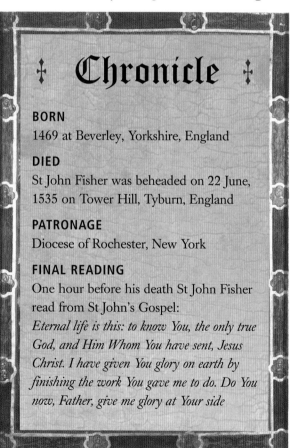

✢ Chronicle ✢

BORN
1469 at Beverley, Yorkshire, England

DIED
St John Fisher was beheaded on 22 June, 1535 on Tower Hill, Tyburn, England

PATRONAGE
Diocese of Rochester, New York

FINAL READING
One hour before his death St John Fisher read from St John's Gospel:
Eternal life is this: to know You, the only true God, and Him Whom You have sent, Jesus Christ. I have given You glory on earth by finishing the work You gave me to do. Do You now, Father, give me glory at Your side

St John the Baptist

John was the son of Zechariah, a Temple priest, and Elizabeth, a cousin of Mary the mother of Jesus. John was therefore a second cousin of Jesus and probably knew him from childhood.

John began his mission of preaching and baptising on the banks of the River Jordan in about AD 24. His ascetic wilderness way of life, living on 'locusts and honey', and his stark message of repentance to escape divine retribution were highly reminiscent of the great Old Testament prophets. In a sense he was the last of the Old Testament prophets.

John urged people to mend their ways as the Messiah was about to arrive: Divine Judgement would shortly follow. To prove their repentance, people underwent a simple ceremony of immersion in the River Jordan, then returned to their ordinary lives, but behaved better. A few decided to commit themselves more deeply to the Baptiser, and became his disciples. Among these were Peter and Andrew, who were to become followers of Jesus, and Jesus himself.

John denounced the incestuous marriage of Herod Antipas and his niece Herodias, and this led to his arrest and imprisonment. His death was brought about by the understandable hatred of Herodias. Herod was delighted with his daughter Salome's dancing at his birthday feast and, when he asked her to name her reward, at her mother's instigation Salome asked for the head of John the Baptist on a platter. Herod sent an executioner to Machaerus on the Dead Sea, where John was imprisoned, and without any kind of trial he was summarily executed by beheading. Jesus had by this time, around AD 27, started work as John's disciple in Judaea, but after John's arrest Jesus went to Galilee, to escape Herod's jurisdiction.

The Gospel version of events tends to play down John the Baptist's importance. By the Fourth Gospel, he is reduced to the voice crying in the wilderness, denying that he is the Messiah. He was nevertheless a major witness to the approach of the Messiah and the Gospels give him a key role in Jesus's life by being his baptiser. The baptism of Jesus by his cousin was marked by a special miraculous sign. The Spirit of God descended on Jesus 'like a dove'. Mark and Matthew describe this as an inward experience that was felt by Jesus alone; Luke conjures up a physical bird that was visible to onlookers. Whatever actually happened on the banks of the Jordan, it marked the historic beginning of Jesus's ministry, his formal anointing as the Messiah heralded by John, and it was the moment when it first became clear what the purpose of Jesus's life was to be.

St Peter

For all the mythic grandeur that came later to surround St Peter – first Bishop of Rome, first Pope, keeper of the keys of Heaven – he was a peasant from the north of Palestine, recognisable in Jerusalem by his rough Galilean accent and regarded by the Sanhedrin as an illiterate. Simon Peter was one of the privileged inner circle of Jesus's disciples. He was a natural leader and often acted as a spokesman for the apostles. It was at Caesarea-Philippi that Simon made his great profession of faith in Jesus. Jesus asked him directly, 'Who do you say I am?' Simon Peter answered, 'You are the Christ, the Son of the living God.' Then Jesus called him Cephas in Hebrew, Petros in Greek, the rock on which he would build his Church.

Following the death of Jesus, Simon Peter became the leader of the disciples. He survived the initial persecution and went on missionary journeys to Lydda, Joppa and Caesarea. When the crucial conference was held in Jerusalem to decide whether gentile converts to Christianity had to convert to Judaism as well, it was James who presided, and Peter threw his weight in favour of the gentiles. Later, in Antioch, Peter seems to have relapsed to a Judaising position and the last mention of him in the New Testament is St Paul's rebuke for this.

Probably, after this rift with St Paul, Peter stayed in Antioch and preached there. But he eventually went to Rome, probably in AD 50, presided over the Church there, and it may even be that Paul sent for him. This late, undocumented phase of Peter's life is surrounded by legend. One story about Peter tells of a contest between the saint and the pagan magician Simon Magus, which has Peter causing the magician to fall to his death. Another story is that at the end of his life he had the opportunity to escape. He reached one of the gates of Rome, where he met Jesus coming in. Peter asked him, 'Lord, where are you going?' Jesus answered, 'To Rome to be crucified again.' Peter was overcome by shame and returned to face his own martyrdom.

By tradition, St Peter suffered martyrdom on the same day, though not in the same place, as St Paul. Again by tradition, he was crucified upside down at his own request, because he felt unworthy to die in the same way as his master. The Church in Rome always regarded him as the first Bishop of Rome and the first Pope; accordingly his remains were buried deep under the high altar of St Peter's Basilica. In the 1950s the bones of a tall, strongly-built old man were found in exactly the expected place.

St Swithun

Chronicle

BORN

c.800 in Wessex, England

DIED

2 July 862

PATRONAGE

Drought relief, churches at Stavenger and Winchester, England

MEMORIAL

2 July; 15 July (translation of relics)

SHRINE

Until its destruction in 1538, the shrine of St Swithun in Winchester Cathedral was among the most popular in medieval England

Swithun was born into an aristocratic family in Hampshire in about 805. He entered the Church and was ordained by Bishop Helmstan of Winchester. Swithun became tutor to King Egbert's son Ethelwulf, who eventually, in 852, made him Bishop of Winchester and his principal adviser on Church matters.

Very little else is known about Swithun. Nothing is known of his personal life, except that his humility prevented him from riding a horse; he went everywhere on foot. It is also recorded that he ordered repair work on many churches in his diocese and built a bridge over the River Itchen.

Just one miracle was reported during his lifetime. A market-woman crossing Swithun's bridge on her way to Winchester market was jostled by a workman. She dropped her basket, broke her eggs and the kindly bishop mended them for her.

Before Swithun died he is said to have asked, out of humility, to be buried outside his church. He died on 2 July 862 and was, as he requested, buried outside Winchester Cathedral on the north side. The cathedral was rebuilt a century later, and then Swithun's remains were transferred to a new grave – inside. On 15 July 971, Swithun's body was reburied in a shrine at the east end of the cathedral. So many miracles were worked at the shrine that the monks became tired of acknowledging people's gratitude.

St Swithun's shrine was a major focus for pilgrims through the middle ages. This only came to an end when the monasteries were dissolved in 1538, and his shrine was destroyed.

St Margaret
of Antioch

Chronicle

BORN
Antioch

DIED
Beheaded by Emperor Diocletian and buried at Antioch

PATRONAGE
Against sterility, childbirth, dying people, escape from devils, exiles, expectant mothers, martyrs, nurses, peasants, people in exile, pregnant women, Queens College Cambridge, safe childbirth, women, women in labour

REPRESENTATION
In the stained glass image (*right*) St Margaret can be seen kneeling with a chain around her neck, but she is also depicted as victorious by holding a cross over a dragon

St Margaret is another of those extraordinary saints who are very well known as names, and who have been venerated for centuries, but about whom almost nothing is known.

St Margaret of Antioch is said to have been the daughter of a pagan priest at Antioch in Pisidia. She was brought up as a Christian by her nurse and, when her father found out, he was extremely angry. He refused to allow her into his house, so she was forced to go and live with her nurse. She had to make her living by looking after sheep.

While Margaret was tending her sheep, she attracted the attention of Olybius, the prefect, who became obsessed with her and wanted her at any cost. If she was free-born he would marry her, if she was a slave he would buy her. She told him that she was free-born but a Christian and that she would not marry him. Olybius had her imprisoned, where the devil appeared to her in the form of a dragon. Margaret was tortured and finally beheaded.

St Margaret was one of the band of cast-iron virgin saints who were so popular in the middle ages. She was also one of the saints who appeared to Joan of Arc, telling her to help the Dauphin to rid France of the English.

St Mary Magdalene

Mary Magdalene is the most enigmatic figure in the story of Jesus. Controversy still rages round her true identity, character and role. She was a contemporary of Jesus who came from a town called Magdala near the Sea of Galilee. The Gospel according to St Luke portrays Mary as a woman afflicted by seven devils, who was cured and afterwards accompanied Jesus on his missionary travels.

Mary Magdalene was one of several women who were not only followers of Jesus but supported him from their own financial resources. The Gospel according to St John tells us that when Jesus was crucified she stood at the foot of the cross with Mary, Jesus's mother, Mary the wife of Cleophas and another woman called Salome. Mark and Matthew mention her as one of a group of women watching from further away. There were evidently differing views about the importance of these female disciples.

It is generally believed that Mary was the unnamed woman, described as 'a sinner', who in an extraordinary gesture of love wept at Jesus's feet, anointed them with expensive oils and wiped them with her hair. Some think she was also the same Mary who was the sister of Lazarus and Martha, but the truth is that the name Mary was a common one and the Gospels make it clear that several women called Mary were involved in the life of Jesus.

Mary Magdalene was present when the body of Jesus was laid in the tomb. She was, most importantly of all, the one who came early on Easter morning to anoint the body and found the tomb empty. She collapsed in tears, then saw someone in the garden nearby. At first she thought it was the gardener, but then realised that it was Jesus himself, risen from the dead. She ran to tell the other disciples, who went to see the empty tomb for themselves.

After that, the canonical (standard) gospels are silent about Mary Magdalene and nothing is known of her history after the Resurrection. In the Greek Church a tradition developed that she travelled with John to Ephesus, where she died and was buried.

The early Church tried to establish that women should take a subordinate role in the Church, in keeping with contemporary practice. To justify this, the pre-eminence of the male disciples during the ministry had to be asserted, and that meant selecting and revising the various narratives of the ministry. Some gospels were completely suppressed, among them the Gospel of Mary, which showed her as a far more important disciple than many of the men.

St Christopher

Chronicle

BORN

Canaan as Offero

DIED

Martyred *c*.250

NAME MEANING

Christ-bearer

REPRESENTATION

In this stained glass window (*right*) St Christopher is depicted as a man with child (Jesus) on his shoulders

PRAYER

Dear Saint, you have inherited a beautiful name – Christbearer – as a result of a wonderful legend that while carrying people across a raging stream you also carried the Child Jesus. Teach us to be true Christbearers to those who do not know him. Protect all drivers who often transport those who bear Christ within them. Amen.

St Christopher died around the year AD 250 during a persecution of Christians. Nothing else is known about him for certain; his reputation and popularity rest on legend.

By tradition or fable he was a Canaanite, and a tall and powerfully built man. He decided to serve the greatest and darkest prince in the world. He had served a king, but found him unsatisfactory, and followed the Devil instead. When on their travels the Devil encountered the Cross, he shrank from it, and Christopher pressed him to explain. When he discovered that 'a man called Christ' was hanged on the cross, Christopher knew that he had found a greater master than the Devil.

A hermit told him he should ferry people across a river. One day he was called out of his hut by a child, 'Christopher, come out and carry me across.' He went out, hoisted the child onto his shoulder, and took him across the river, though the river rose higher and higher and the child grew heavier and heavier.

Christopher told the child he had put him in great danger, and the child told him, 'You have carried all the world on your shoulder, and him that created it. I am Jesus.' Christopher stuck his staff in the ground and the next day it had taken root, bearing flowers, leaves and dates.

The image of Christopher gently bearing the Christ child across the river is one of the most potent Christian images. That image has become a talisman for travellers, and Christopher himself is the patron saint of travellers.

St James
the Great

✝ Chronicle ✝

BORN

Not documented

DIED

Martyred at the hands of King Herod Agrippa in 44 at Jerusalem. Shrine at Santiago de Compostela, in north-west Spain

PRAYER

O Glorious Saint James, because of your fervor and generosity Jesus chose you to witness his glory on the Mount and his agony in the Garden. Obtain for us strength and consolation in the unending struggles of this life. Help us to follow Christ constantly and generously, to be victors over all our difficulties, and to receive the crown of glory in heaven. Amen

St James the Great was the son of Zebedee and Salome, the brother of St John and a cousin of Jesus. James and John were partners with Andrew and Simon Peter, and were called by Jesus to be his Apostles at the same time. Following the miraculous catch of fish in the Sea of Galilee, which proved that Jesus was a great worker of wonders, they gave up everything to follow him.

James belonged to the privileged inner circle of disciples who witnessed several key moments in the life of Jesus. They were there when Jesus raised Jairus's daughter from the dead. They witnessed the Transfiguration. They were with Jesus at his arrest in the Garden of Gethsemane.

Some fourteen years after the Crucifixion, Herod Agrippa ordered the arrest of James and Peter. James was put to death with the sword. His accuser was so profoundly moved by James's behaviour at his trial that he confessed that he was a Christian, and he too was led away to be executed.

According to a medieval legend, James preached for a time in Spain and when he was beheaded his body was placed on board a ship at Jaffa, set adrift, and it eventually reached Spain. The place where his body was buried was revealed in a vision in 800 and the remains were transferred to Compostela, which became a major pilgrimage focus. St James became the patron saint of Spain.

St Anne

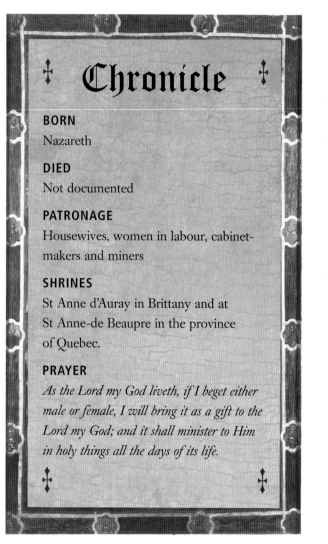

Chronicle

BORN
Nazareth

DIED
Not documented

PATRONAGE
Housewives, women in labour, cabinet-makers and miners

SHRINES
St Anne d'Auray in Brittany and at St Anne-de Beaupre in the province of Quebec.

PRAYER
As the Lord my God liveth, if I beget either male or female, I will bring it as a gift to the Lord my God; and it shall minister to Him in holy things all the days of its life.

St Anne, or Anna, was the mother of the Virgin Mary, and therefore the grand-mother of Jesus. She was the wife of Joachim. In reality, nothing is known for certain of either of Mary's parents, and the names Anne and Joachim have been assigned on the strength of tradition only. They first appear in an early apocryphal text called the *Protoevangelium of James,* which gives an account, among other things, of Mary's birth.

Anne was said to have been born in Nazareth, the daughter of a nomad called Akar. She married Joachim at the age of 20 but was still childless at 40 when she was visited by an angel who told her that she would bear a child.

A cult of St Anne was under way by the sixth century and became very popular in the middle ages. The relationship between Anne and Joachim was seen as a perfect model for Christian marriage, without the obvious drawback involved in setting up as a model the marriage of Mary and Joseph, with its pregnancy during betrothal.

In paintings, St Anne is often shown with Mary and Jesus, in the benign supporting role of the perfect grandmother.

St Samson of Dol

S t Samson was a contemporary of King Arthur. He was a scourging prelate, inveighing fearlessly against wrong-doing wherever he came across it, storming sarcastically against kings, queens, judges and priests – and apparently with impunity. Sixth century holy men seem to have had a licence to be outspoken, rather like the fools or jesters that dark age kings kept beside them. The narrative of St Samson's life nevertheless shows that some of his contemporaries found his abrasive self-righteousness too strong to take, and asked Samson to move on. He showed the coarseness of the pioneering spirit.

Samson's father was a landowner in south-west Wales and a companion of the king of Demetia. The suggestion that Samson should attend St Illtud's school at Llantwit came from 'a learned master who lived in the north', probably Maucennus, Bishop of Whithorn, who is known to have visited Demetia at about the right time. By the time he was 15, Samson was already very learned, and he was ordained priest and deacon at an unusually young age by Bishop Dubricius. This created jealousy among Illtud's nephews, who feared that Samson might succeed as the school's head when Illtud retired and so deprive them of their inheritance. Possibly because of this ill-feeling, Samson was transferred to another of Illtud's monasteries, newly set up by Piro on Caldey Island.

On Caldey Island, Samson astonished the other monks with his scholarship and austerity – he fasted severely. In the winter a message came that his father was seriously ill. Piro persuaded Samson that he should go. On the way, he encountered a distraught old woman waving a trident and shrieking. It turned out that she was the only member of her family left alive, and she could not leave the wood where her husband had died. In her ravings, she knocked a man down. Samson's response was to call on God to stop her from doing any more harm and she fell down dead. To modern eyes, Samson's behaviour seems cruel and inappropriate, and so it seemed to Dubricius, who travelled to Caldey to investigate the incident. Whatever reservations Dubricius had about Samson, he acquitted him and confirmed his stewardship of the Caldey monastery.

Samson hungered for hardship and was in truth more suited to the hermetic life than the monastic. After a visit to Ireland and a brief return to Caldey, he left for an abandoned fort beside the River Severn, then went to live in a cave at Stackpole. He was guided by visions, and his inner voices directed him to cross to the monastery of Landocco founded by Docco at St Kew in Cornwall, which was already old when Samson arrived there.

The abbot of Landocco, Iuniavus, told Samson plainly that he was not welcome there; Samson's standards were too high for his monks. 'We might feel condemned by your superior merit. You had better go to Europe.' Samson was stupefied, made his way across Cornwall to 'the Southern Sea', and sailed to Brittany to become Bishop of the kingdom of Jonas of Dumnonie. For the rest of his life he was based at Dol in King Jonas's kingdom.

Before Samson left St Kew, he came upon a crowd of subjects of Count Gwedian celebrating pagan rites at an unidentified standing stone. Samson dispersed the crowd and carved a cross on the stone with his pocket knife, an ad hoc example of the Christianisation of pagan monoliths which was very common in Brittany.

Samson died an old man in Brittany in 565.

St Germanus

Chronicle

BORN

c.378 at Auxerre, France

ALSO KNOWN AS

Germain of Auxerre

DIED

Died of natural causes on 31 July, 448 in Ravenna, Italy. After desecration of his shrine by the Huguenots in 1567, it is thought that his remains now lie in Saint Marion Abbey

PATRONAGE

Auxerre, France

REPRESENTATION

St Germanus is usually represented as a Bishop carrying a knife as in the stained glass window on the opposite page

German or Germanus was brought up as a Christian at Auxerre, where he was born in AD 378. He entered the Imperial service, in which he achieved promotion to a high position; he became one of six governors of Gaul, where he had responsibility for governing Brittany.

Germanus's main pastime was hunting and he used to hang up the heads of the animals he killed in the branches of a tree in Auxerre. This scandalised his Christian neighbours as hanging up trophy heads – whether of beasts or human enemies – was a pagan practice. The local bishop in the end had the trophy tree felled while Germanus was away, to his great annoyance.

When Germanus was forty, the bishop ordained him priest by force, shortly afterwards making him a bishop. This transformed Germanus completely. From then on he devoted himself to promoting the Christian cause.

In 429, the British bishops became alarmed at the spread of heresy and sent for help. In response to this, Germanus of Auxerre and Lupus of Troyes were sent to assist. There was a conference at St Albans at which Germanus and Lupus met the heretic priests in a confrontational debate, and which Germanus and Lupus won.

King Vortigern was at that time king of Powys, a kingdom that sprawled across central Wales and the western part of central England. Vortigern gave Germanus the impression that he was in charge of a much larger area, so he was probably the southern British over-king.

While in Britain in 429, Germanus became involved in an unexpected adventure. Wales was invaded by Picts and Scots. The spirit of the Britons was broken by many earlier defeats, and they called on the charismatic bishops to inspire them. Germanus and Lupus marched with the soldiers, taking every opportunity to preach and pray with them. As Easter approached they even built a rough wattle church to celebrate the festival in style. As the enemy approached, Germanus was overwhelmed by an instinct to take over the leadership of the army. He announced that he wanted to do this and the army agreed. He organised an ambush for the invaders in a Welsh valley. As the enemy approached, Germanus signalled to his troops, who all shouted 'Alleluia!' The shout echoed round the valley and the enemy fled in panic. This battle was remembered as the Alleluia Victory and it probably restored central Wales to Vortigern's control.

Germanus returned to France. He revisited Britain 17 years later when there was another revival of heresy, but was almost immediately recalled to defend the Armoricans (Bretons) who were accused of rebellion. He travelled to Ravenna to plead their cause with the Emperor. He was received in Ravenna with great respect and died there on 31 July 448.

Germanus's career is of special interest in giving us a glimpse of what was happening in Britain in the fifth century, an otherwise very poorly documented phase of British history.

St Ignatius Loyala

Ignatius Loyola, or more properly Inigo Lopez de Loyola, was born in 1491 into a noble Basque family, one of thirteen children, and was brought up in the Castle of Loyola. He had been a courtier, lover and soldier when a bullet in the leg at the siege of Pamplona changed the course of his life. As he lay recovering from his wound he was given a book about saints and a *Life of Christ* to read. He wanted to imitate the saints.

When he was well enough, though still with a limp, he went on a pilgrimage to Jerusalem, which he eventually reached in 1523. When he returned to Spain, he was determined to become a student, though at two universities he got into trouble with the Inquisition; what he said about religion made the authorities suspect that he was a heretic. At Alcala he was imprisoned for 42 days and forbidden to talk about 'novelties'. He retorted that he could not see how talking about Jesus was a novelty. He spent seven years at the University of Paris, where a small group of disciples gathered round him. Francis Xavier was one of them. No clear plan was formulated, except a common instinct to abandon earthly ties and free themselves to serve God. Ignatius and six companions vowed to do this in the Chapel of St Denis de Montmartre. A pilgrimage to Jerusalem was to be followed by a visit to Rome where they would put themselves at the Pope's service. Ignatius Loyola made his way to Venice in 1535, where he acquired several companions or disciples, and once again found himself accused of heresy. It was said that he had escaped from Spain because of heresy charges and been burned in effigy in Paris.

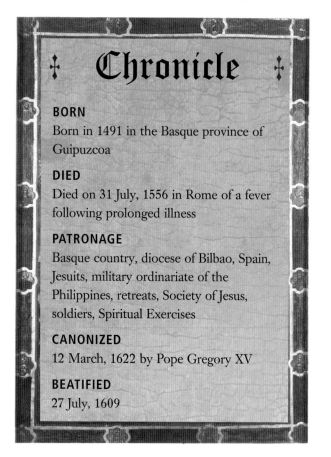

Chronicle

BORN
Born in 1491 in the Basque province of Guipuzcoa

DIED
Died on 31 July, 1556 in Rome of a fever following prolonged illness

PATRONAGE
Basque country, diocese of Bilbao, Spain, Jesuits, military ordinariate of the Philippines, retreats, Society of Jesus, soldiers, Spiritual Exercises

CANONIZED
12 March, 1622 by Pope Gregory XV

BEATIFIED
27 July, 1609

The trip to Jerusalem was too difficult to organise, but they put to the Pope a plan to form a community, which was approved in 1540. This Society of Jesus was modelled on the old military orders, reflecting Ignatius Loyola's military experience. The head of the Society, to whom absolute obedience was due, was to be called the General. Ignatius was unanimously elected the order's first general. He settled in Rome, concerning himself with the conversion of Jews, the rescue of fallen women and the care of orphans.

Ignatius believed strongly in the value of education, founding first the Roman College, then a string of schools and colleges all over Europe. He also organised missionary expeditions much further afield. Francis Xavier was sent to India and Japan, while other members of the Society went to China, the Congo and Brazil.

The Society of Jesus was well-known internationally by the time of Ignatius Loyola's death, and the story of Ignatius's life is mainly seen as the story of the birth and growth of the Society of Jesus. Its members were to become known as Jesuits. Ignatius Loyola was taken ill early in 1556, when he resigned, leaving the Society in the charge of three fathers. He died suddenly on 31 July, 1556 and was canonized in 1622.

St Oswald

Oswald, the great seventh century King of Northumbria, was the first of the English royal saints. He was a member of the royal family of Bernicia and when he was excluded from the Bernician throne in the reign of King Edwin he took refuge in Scotland. Edwin ruled Northumbria, which incorporated the two old kingdoms of Bernicia and Deira.

The pagan King Caedwalla ravaged Northumbria for two years, killing Edwin and his sons. Oswald then distinguished himself as a warrior by defeating Caedwalla at the great Battle of Heavenfield in 635. He turned this historic occasion into something of a crusade, raising a cross with his own hands before going into battle and calling on his troops to kneel and pray in front of it for victory over 'the proud and fierce enemy'. It was the clearest statement that in Oswald's eyes this was a holy war. The monks at nearby Hexham Abbey were afterwards, on the eve of the anniversary of Oswald's death, to go to the place where the cross was raised, to pray for the dead king's soul. Later they built a church on the spot. These were the first Christian monuments to be raised in Bernicia, in North-East England.

One of Oswald's first acts on being restored to his kingdom was to send to the holy island of Iona for a bishop, so that the Christian message could be spread among his people. Aidan eventually responded by travelling to Northumbria, where he was rewarded by Oswald's warm support for his mission.

Quite apart from being a saint, Oswald was very successful as a secular leader. He reunited Bernicia and Deira to re-create Northumbria, and even established overlordship over Picts, Scots and the rest of the English, earning himself the title bretwalda, over-king of Britain.

After reigning for only eight years, Oswald was killed in battle at Maserfield, which is thought to have been on the site of modern Oswestry. When the king was killed, he was cut to pieces in a barbaric ritual. His head and limbs were nailed to a tree, which became known as 'Oswald's tree'. The grisly remains were left there for a full year before Oswin took them down. The head was taken for burial at Lindisfarne, and the arms and body to Bamburgh.

Many prayed to Oswald for help, and many claimed miracles. The best documented miracle happened in Sussex in 681. The monastery founded at Selsey by Wilfrid was afflicted by an epidemic. Many of the monks died, and the epidemic only ended after a little boy at the monastery had a vision in which St Peter told him that the plague would end, thanks to the intervention of King Oswald, though the boy himself would die. The day of the vision was the anniversary of Oswald's death and things turned out just as St Peter foretold.

St Dominic

Chronicle

BORN
1170 at Calaroga, Burgos, Old Castile

DIED
4 August 1221 at Bologna

PATRONAGE
Astronomers, astronomy, falsely accused people, scientists

CANONIZED
13 July 1234 by Pope Gregory IX at Rieti, Italy

PRAYER
Wonderful Saintly Founder of the eloquent Order of Preachers and friend of Saint Francis of Assisi, you were a fiery defender of the Faith and a fighter against the darkness of heresy. You resembled a great star that shone close to the world and pointed to the Light which was Christ. Help astronomers to study the stars and admire their wonderful Maker, proclaiming: 'Give glory to God in the highest'. Amen

Dominic was born at Calaroga in Old Castile in 1170 and was the founder of the Dominican order of friar-preachers. Before Dominic's time the ruling principle had been separation from the world, in order to join Christ. Dominic and later Francis, too, advocated saving the world not by renouncing it but by mingling and engaging with it.

Dominic was educated at the University of Palencia, where he spent some twelve years in theological study. He is said to have sold his clothes and books to give money to the poor. On one occasion he was allegedly prepared to offer himself in slavery, in order to release a man who had been captured by the Moors.

At the age of 25 he became Canon of Osma, his native diocese, where he became famous for the extreme length of his prayers. He spent whole nights in church in prayer. The years between 1195 and 1205 are full of fabulous stories about missions to the Moors, but in fact Dominic stayed at Osma, frequently preaching in the cathedral. It was on his visit to Languedoc in southern France in 1206 that he had the idea of founding his new order. He was sent there specifically by Pope Innocent III to preach among the Albigensian heretics, which he did for ten years. He became aware early on that it was mainly weapons and persecution that were used against the heretics, and that few attempts other than his own were being made to teach and convert them. He was sickened by the massacre of the heretics in the years following 1208, when the papal legate was murdered.

Dominic established the Rosary as a method of giving clear and simple teaching, and to provide simple, spiritual exercises for people who were unable to read prayer-books.

In 1215, he won permission from Innocent III to set up his new order. His preachers were to be independent of bishops, though Innocent hesitated about this. The Dominican order was hugely successful and spread rapidly. In five years there were Dominican converts in Italy, Spain, France, Germany and Poland, comprising over 500 friars and 60 friaries.

In 1221, he fell ill at Venice. He had planned to preach to the heathen in Russia, but he was worn out by the demands of his austere lifestyle. Now he knew he was dying, and asked to be taken to one of his own monasteries at Bologna, where he died on 4 August. Dominic was a humble, devout and modest man. Once, when he and his followers arrived late at a monastery and found the monks had already gone to bed, he said, 'Don't wake them. We can sleep on the steps.' His personality was quite different from the stern, uncompromising face that his order was to acquire in decades to come, Dominic himself was warm, generous, moderate, rather soft-hearted and extremely likeable.

St Laurence

Laurence was Spanish, born in the country three miles outside the town of Huesca, still known as Loretto in Laurence's honour. He was educated at Saragossa and Genoa, where he befriended Sixtus. Laurence was Archdeacon of Rome during the persecution of Christians under the Emperor Valerian in AD 258. He watched his friend Sixtus, also his bishop, being led away to execution and asked, 'Why do you leave me, father? Should the priest go to the sacrifice without his attendant deacon?' The Bishop answered that he would soon follow.

As keeper of the church treasure, Laurence was ordered to produce it by the authorities. He asked for a day in which collect it, and then visited the poorest quarters of the city. He returned to the tribunal accompanied by a crowd of beggars and cripples. 'These,' he said, 'are the Church's treasures.'

The authorities ordered Laurence to be roasted on a gridiron. It was said that he showed no sign of suffering during this awful martyrdom, only speaking to the executioners to say, 'Turn me, I am done on this side!' Laurence became Rome's patron martyr. In the cemetery outside the gates of Rome the Emperor Constantine ordered the building of a basilica over his tomb. In England alone there are 280 churches bearing his name. Laurence is usually depicted in art as a calm and angelic young man dressed as a deacon; his emblems are a book and a gridiron.

Chronicle

BORN

Near Huesca, Spain *c.*225

DIED

Martyred on 10 August, 258, by burning on a red-hot gridiron

REPRESENTATION

St Laurence is usually depicted holding a gridiron and wearing a dalmatic (a liturgical vestmest worn at Mass)

READING

With the robe of joyfulness, alleluya,
Our Lord hath this day clothed His soldier,
* Laurence.*
May Thy faithful's joyous assemblage clap their
* hands*
More cheerfully than they have heretofore

St Clare

✠ Chronicle ✠

BORN
16 July 1194 at Assisi, Italy

DIED
11 August, 1253 of natural causes

PATRONAGE
Embroiderers, eye disease, eyes, gilders, goldsmiths, gold workers, good weather, laundry workers, needle workers, Santa Clara Indian Pueblo, telegraphs, telephones, television

CANONIZED
26 September 1255 by Pope Alexander IV

READING
Go forth in peace, for you have followed the good road. Go forth without fear, for he who created you has made you holy, has always protected you, and loves you as a mother. Blessed be you, my God, for having created me.

Clare Offreducia was born in 1194 into an aristocratic family. She dismayed her parents at the age of 12 when she refused to marry, and even more a few years later when she ran away from home to become a nun; after hearing St Francis preach. She joined the Benedictine nuns in a convent at Bastia. Clare's younger sister, Agnes, also ran away and joined her.

In 1215, Francis offered Clare a house in Assisi, where she became abbess of the first community of women living under the austere Franciscan rule. After their father died, Clare and Agnes were joined at Assisi by their mother and another sister, Beatrice. Clare obtained a charter from Pope Innocent III which ensured absolute poverty without ownership of any property and living entirely on charity. Her order became known as the Poor Clare order, which spread throughout Europe.

Legend has it that she once saw in a vision a Christmas service she was too ill to attend, and this led to her adoption (in 1958) as the patron saint of television.

Clare spent her entire life at Assisi, where she became famous for her meditativeness, holiness and wisdom. She saved Assisi from attack by Frederick II, when his soldiers fled at the sight of Clare on the city walls, holding up the Sacrament. Clare died in 1253 and was canonized only two years later. Her order continues to this day, preserving the ideals that inspired both Clare and her mentor, St Francis.

Mary the Virgin

The Virgin Mary, mother of Jesus, is an icon of unfailing tenderness and motherliness. She is the mother of Jesus, and when she was visited by the angel Gabriel to be told that she had been chosen to bear God's son, she was engaged to be married to Joseph. An angel then visited Joseph in a dream to tell him not to be afraid, but to take Mary as his wife, which he did. Mary and Joseph lived in Nazareth in Galilee, but shortly before her baby was due to be born they were called to Bethlehem, approximately 90 miles away, to be recorded in a census. They undertook this journey with Mary riding on the back of a donkey, but when they got to Bethlehem they could find no shelter for the night. The inns were crowded so Mary and Joseph were directed to a stable. During the night, the baby was born and was placed in the manger for a crib. Joseph had been instructed by the angel to name the baby Jesus.

Little else is known of the Virgin Mary. She apparently went back to Nazareth, where she stayed for thirty years. She did accompany Jesus on his journey to Jerusalem, at the age of twelve, when he spent time with the teachers in the temple, and she was also there at the marriage in Cana, when Jesus turned the water into wine. She is also recorded as having attended some of the events of Jesus's public ministry along with his disciples.

One of the final, and most significant, reports of Mary's appearance is at Jesus's crucifixion. According to John, this was one of the most tender moments between mother and dying son. It was then that Jesus committed her to the care of John.

Mary is not mentioned as having seen Jesus after the Crucifixion, though she is mentioned in the Acts of the Apostles as continuing to pray with her son's disciples.

No more is contained in the Church's official documents. There is no mention of her death. Legends and traditions abound. Some say she died at Jerusalem; some that she accompanied St John to Ephesus and died there. The Feast of the Assumption, 15 August, is the traditional date of her death, and there is a medieval story that when the Apostles opened her tomb they found her body gone; instead it was filled with flowers. This accompanied the idea that like her son she had ascended into heaven. One curious feature of Mary is that she is always portrayed as colourless, leaving it open to worshippers to project their own ideals of womanhood and motherhood onto her. She is eternally sweet, beautiful, tender, and caring.

St Helena

Helena, who lived from about AD 240 to 327, was the daughter of an innkeeper yet she married a general, Constantius, who became emperor in 292, and she also became the mother of a Roman emperor - Constantine the Great, the first Christian emperor. It is said that she became a Christian through the influence of her son. At the age of eighty she made a pilgrimage to Jerusalem.

Helena gave large sums of money to the poor, and used her influence to have prisoners released and exiles recalled. She is also said to have built churches on the sites of the Crucifixion, Resurrection and Ascension. It was during her visit to the Holy Land that Helena discovered the wood of the true Cross, the cross on which Jesus was crucified. According to the story, she found the three crosses on which Jesus and the two thieves were crucified and was at first unable to tell which was the cross on which Jesus died. Helena experimented. She asked for slivers of wood to be taken from each cross and taken to the bedside of a sick woman. Two of the pieces of wood had no effect, but the third brought about a complete recovery, so that had to be from the 'true' Cross.

The story is corroborated by a wooden plaque, treated as a relic in Rome for many centuries, which may be the actual label that was fixed to the cross, announcing that Jesus was the King of the Jews. It was taken to Rome around the reign of Constantine.

Constantine was drawn into the rediscovery of the tomb of Jesus by Bishop Makarios of Jerusalem, who asked the emperor's permission 'to destroy the Temple of Venus in the quest for the tomb of Christ.' When he removed the rubble, Makarios staggeringly found the tomb straight away, 'against all hope', 150 feet north-west of Golgotha. He knew from the Gospel story that the two sites would be close together. This is the tomb still venerated today as the Holy Sepulchre. Constantine ordered a church to be built covering both sites; it was dedicated in 335. Helena is said to have found the true cross about 100 feet east of Golgotha; this site too is incorporated into the Church of the Holy Sepulchre.

Chronicle

BORN
Around 240

DIED
Died of natural causes in 327

PATRONAGE
Archaeologists, converts, difficult marriages, divorced people, empresses

REPRESENTATION
St Helena is normally depicted holding a large wooden cross. She has also been represented as royalty, wearing a crown

St Bernard
of Clairvaux

FEAST DAY: 20 AUGUST

BORN

1090 at Fontaines-les-Dijon,
Burgundy, France

DIED

Died of natural causes on
20 August, 1153 at Clairvaux

PRAYER

*O God, by whose grace thy
servant Bernard of Clairvaux,
Enkindled with the fire of thy
love, became a burning and a
shining light in thy Church:
Grant that we also may be
aflame with the spirit of love and
discipline, and may ever walk
before thee as children of light;
through Jesus Christ our Lord,
who with thee, in the unity of the
Holy Spirit, liveth and reigneth,
one God, now and for ever*

Bernard was born near Dijon in 1090, the son of a Burgundian knight. He was a thoughtful boy and seemed destined to become a scholar, but he decided at the age of 22 to become a Cistercian monk at Citeaux. He was persuasive, and he managed to press an uncle and four of his brothers to join him. He urged men to renounce the world with such vigour that mothers hid sons, wives hid husbands and men hid susceptible friends.

Bernard was a fine-looking man with a winning way; he was both well-mannered and eloquent. Citeaux was a monastery that strictly followed the Benedictine rule. Its monks had just one meal a day and never ate meat, fish or eggs. But the rule of St Benedict was not strict enough for Bernard, who made it still more austere. The abbot, an Englishman called Stephen Harding, chose Bernard to set up a daughter house. He set off in June 1115 with 12 other monks to found a monastery in a gloomy valley at a place that would become famous as Clairvaux.

Bernard spent the next 15 years at Clairvaux, preaching, studying, teaching, and his fame gradually spread throughout Europe. His correspondence became more and more voluminous, as more people sought his advice. In 1130, he became entangled in the dispute over the election to the papacy. The claim of Innocent II was disputed by an anti-pope called Anacletus II, and Bernard emerged as Innocent's champion. He persuaded both Louis VI of France and Henry I of England to acknowledge Innocent as pope – and it was Bernard's personal influence that persuaded the emperor to do the same when they met at Liege.

From that moment on, Bernard was unquestionably the most powerful man in Europe. Popes and kings relied on his support, and he was forthright in his rebukes to wrong-doers. His own monks went on to occupy important positions; one became Archbishop of York, another became Pope. He was equally influential among ordinary people. When he passed along a road, farm labourers and shepherds hurried from the fields to the roadside to receive his blessing.

In 1146, he was instructed by the Pope to preach the Second Crusade. This he did at Easter, in front of the King and Queen of France and a huge assembly of knights and peasants. His appearance and speech were profoundly moving, provoking a great roar of 'Crosses, crosses!' which he then distributed. For the next few months he toured France and Germany urging people to go on the crusade. The Second Crusade was, nevertheless, a complete failure, and a huge personal disappointment to Bernard himself.

Bernard was a great force for religious orthodoxy. He supported the orthodox theologians in their attack on Peter Abelard, whose novel speculations excited suspicion and hostility. It was out of thinking like Bernard's that the Inquisition would grow.

At 62 Bernard had aged prematurely, probably because of the excessively austere rule by which he lived. He accepted that he was going to die and ridiculed his monks when they prayed for his recovery. He died in 1153, one of the most influential people of the middle ages.

St Louis

Chronicle

BORN
25 April, 1214 at Poissy, France

DIED
Died of fever on 25 August, 1270 in Tunis, Algeria. His remains, which were held at Saint Denis, Paris, were destroyed in 1793 during the French Revolution

CANONIZED
11 August, 1297 by Pope Boniface VIII

NAME MEANING
Famous warrior

READING
In order to avoid discord, never contradict anyone except in case of sin or some danger to a neighbour; and when necessary to contradict others, do it with tact and not with temper.

Louis IX succeeded to the French throne in 1226. Unusually for a medieval king, he was just, conscientious and not at all greedy for power. When offered the imperial crown by the pope, he declined it. He was devout but in common with other Christians of his time thought the only way to deal with non-Christians ('infidels') was to put them to the sword. He was a tough and capable king, a strong enforcer of justice; during his reign, thieves and murderers were swiftly executed. He conscientiously wished the best for his people, even telling his eldest son that he would rather see a Scot ruling France than his own son ruling badly.

In 1243, when recovering from a serious illness, Louis organised a crusade to the Holy Land. This was against the better judgement of his courtiers, but they went with him out of loyalty. He was an impressive sight, towering above those around him, a gilded helmet on his head and a German sword in his hand.

During the crusade he was captured and threatened with torture and death, but still he refused to take any oath that brought dishonour on the Christian faith. When plague struck his army, he supervised the burial of the dead and helped to carry putrefying corpses.

When he returned to France, it was to an even more ascetic and rigorous life than before. In 1267, he decided against all advice to launch another crusade. The army got no further than Tunis when King Louis fell ill; he died in August 1270.

St Augustine of Hippo

Augustine was born in the small town of Tagaste in Numidia in Roman North Africa, where he was brought up in the Christian faith by his mother, Monica. As a youth, Augustine was keenly intelligent but also passionate and wilful. His behaviour bordered on the pagan, yet the Christian message was imprinted in his mind. Later he reminisced about the sins of his youth. One small crime stuck in his mind – the theft of some pears from a neighbour's tree close to his father's vineyard. It was minor enough, but the adult Augustine was ashamed of the theft and the wantonness of it; he and his friends had fed the pears to some pigs.

He went to Carthage university to study to become a rhetorician. During his studies he came across a book by Cicero about the pursuit of wisdom, and this made him dissatisfied with rhetoric, the art of making the worse appear the better reason. Cicero's book, now lost, changed the course of Augustine's life. He turned to the Bible, but was repelled by what he saw as the vulgarity of its style and also by the questionable morality of much that it contained. After that, Augustine explored the Manichaean philosophy, which taught that the human body was in itself evil; he found this too unsatisfactory, as he did the philosophy of Plato. He even dipped into astrology.

When he was 29, Augustine went to Rome, then two years later to Milan, where he fell under the spell of the great Ambrose, whom he heard preach every Sunday. Ambrose gradually overcame the various objections that Augustine had felt towards Christianity. As he gradually became converted, the immorality of his lifestyle dawned on him and he became deeply depressed. In the end he flung himself down under a fig tree, sobbing, 'Why not now? Why not make this the end of my vile behaviour?' He seemed to hear a voice: 'Take and read.' He took up a Bible and opened it at random. His eyes fell on the passage, 'Not in rioting, not in chambering and wantonness, not in strife nor envy. . .' He followed the instruction to go with Christ.

Augustine was baptised in 386, became a priest at Hippo in 391, and bishop in 395. He became a reformed character, turning his house into a monastery. He eventually died on 28 August 430.

The volatile and mercurial Augustine wrote prolifically, his essays fill eleven volumes. Probably no other writer has had more influence on the development of Christian doctrine than Augustine. Where his teacher, Ambrose, moved the minds of his hearers, Augustine moved their hearts. For hundreds of years, he was the dominant influence on the West. Even in the Reformation, Protestants turned to Augustine's writings for justification. They were where Calvin found his doctrine of predestination. The intensely personal and passionate nature of the *Confessions*, easily the best known of his works, explains why it remains one of the springs of Christian devotional life right up to the present day. It powerfully describes a man struggling to come to terms with the raw frailties of his human nature.

✝ Chronicle ✝

BORN
13 November, 354 at Tagaste, a provincial Roman city in North Africa

DIED
28 August, 430 during the siege of Hippo

CANONIZED
12 March, 1622 by Pope Gregory XV

READING
Beloved Saint of our age, you were at first wholly human-centered and attached to false teachings. Finally converted through God's grace, you became a praying theologian – God-centered, God-loving, God-preaching. Help theologians in their study of revealed truth. Let them always follow the Church Magisterium as they strive to communicate traditional teachings in a form that will appeal and make sense to the world today. Amen

St Aidan

Aidan was a Scot of Irish origin, a monk of Iona, or Hy as it was then called. King Oswald of Northumbria in north-east England asked for a monk to be sent from Iona to his kingdom. When the missionary returned to Iona, he reported to the assembled monks that he had been unable to achieve anything because the Northumbrians were so stubborn.

Aidan said, 'You were more severe on your unlearned audience than you should have been. You should have fed them with the milk of easy doctrine at first, so that they were nourished by degrees with the word of God.' The other monks decided that Aidan should go instead.

In 635 Aidan stayed on Lindisfarne, an island off the Northumberland coast separated by three miles of sea for eight hours a day. But even Lindisfarne with its causeway was not lonely enough for Aidan's prayerful retreats, and he often withdrew to the lonely Farne Islands.

With the support of Oswald and visiting Irish missionaries, Aidan made rapid progress in converting the people, not least because he and his followers always practised what they preached. Whenever Aidan met pagans he invited them to become Christians; whenever he met Christians he spurred them on to do good works. In the spirit of the age, Aidan was not afraid to rebuke the rich and powerful, but he was also gentle with those who needed tender handling.

He was famed for his charity to the poor. When Oswald's successor Oswin gave him a valuable horse, Aidan promptly gave it to a beggar who met him and asked for alms. The king was irritated and said that something of lower value would have been more appropriate. Aidan's cryptic reply was; 'Is that foal of a mare of more value than the Son of God?' Oswin was persuaded that he had been wrong, and asked Aidan to forgive him.

Aidan was a charismatic figure and miracles were attributed to him. He was said to have saved the Northumbrian royal stronghold of Bamburgh when it was besieged by King Penda of Mercia. Bamburgh was on the point of being destroyed by fire. Aidan was at that moment in retreat on the Farne Islands. As he watched the flames and smoke being carried over the walls by the wind, he lifted his eyes to Heaven and prayed: 'Lord, see what harm Penda is doing!' The wind changed direction and the flames were halted.

In August 651, Aidan was taken ill and died at the royal fortress of Bamburgh. His body was taken to Lindisfarne for burial.

St Giles

Chronicle

BORN
Athens, Greece

DIED
*c.*710-724 in France

PATRONAGE
Beggars, blacksmiths, breast cancer, breast feeding, cancer patients, cripples, disabled people, Edinburgh Scotland, epilepsy, fear of night, forests, handicapped people, hermits, horses, insanity, lepers, mental illness, noctiphobics, physically challenged people, paupers, poor people, rams, spur makers, sterility and woods

REPRESENTATION
He is usually represented with a hind and in the picture opposite he appears wounded by an arrow which was intended for the hind

Giles was an Athenian who stayed with Caesarius, Bishop of Arles, on his way to Rome. After that Giles became a hermit, living near the mouth of the River Rhone and living off herbs and the milk of a hind. Flavius, the King of the Goths, was out hunting one day and followed the hind to Giles's cave. The hermit appeared and was wounded by an arrow intended for the deer. Flavius dismounted, heard that the hind was Giles's constant companion, and ordered that they were to be left alone.

Fascinated, the king visited Giles several times subsequently, and the hermit persuaded him to build a monastery. The king agreed only on condition that Giles would be its first abbot. Giles reluctantly agreed.

It was said that Giles prayed that his wound would not heal, saying, 'My strength is made perfect in weakness.' St Giles accordingly became the patron saint of cripples and beggars. He was an immensely popular saint in England in the middle ages, when more than 150 churches were dedicated to him. Because of the church dedications, there are also many streets that bear his name.

St Gregory the Great

It was St Gregory, as Pope Gregory, who commissioned St Augustine to travel to England and convert the English to Christianity. Gregory belonged to a rich and aristocratic Roman family, and was trained as a lawyer. Even while practising law he showed signs of great devotion. When his father died, he inherited enough money to found six Benedictine monasteries in Sicily and a seventh in Rome. It was in this seventh monastery, St Andrew's, that he himself then became a novice, giving up the law to become a monk.

He led a rigorously austere life and suffered for the rest of his life with stomach pains. Shortly after he became a monk he saw some boys for sale in the slave market. He was struck by their white skins and blond hair and enquired who they were. He was told they were Angles (English) to which he replied: 'Not Angles, but angels' (*Non Angli, sed angeli*). Where were they from? Deira (North-East England), he was told. 'From the wrath (*de ira*) of God they must be delivered.' Gregory went to the Pope to get leave to go to England on a mission, but he had been gone only three days when he was asked to return to Rome, because of his popularity there.

In 590, against his will, he was made pope. He was reluctant because he knew the office would constrain him, but he was a very conscientious and wise administrator. No detail was too small for him to consider. He wrote books and even found time to coach a choir himself. He reformed church music, standardising the music for services; the haunting melodies he advocated as suitable for the various bible texts are still known as 'Gregorian' chants.

Gregory himself never went to England as a missionary. He sent Augustine (of Canterbury) instead and supported him with books, vestments, relics, back-up missionaries and plenty of advice. Whenever Augustine was in difficulties he wrote to Gregory, who responded with letters giving detailed and intensely practical advice. Augustine was in favour of destroying the pagan sanctuaries, but Gregory's advice was cautious and wise. Augustine should take the pagan temples over gradually, so as not to disturb the local people's habit of attending ceremonies; it was a better way of winning them round to Christian worship.

Gregory's health was never good. Towards the end of his life he said, 'A kind of fire seems to pervade my whole body; to live is pain.' Gregory the Great died on 12 March 604. For a hundred years or more after that, he was fondly remembered by English clerics, who wrote the first biographies of Gregory, as the father of the church in England.

St Cyprian

† Chronicle †

BORN
190 in Carthage, North Africa

DIED
Beheaded 14 September 258 in Carthage, North Africa

PATRONAGE
Algeria, North Africa

PRAYER
Most gracious Father, bless with your special care all penitentiaries and homes of refuge. Look with pity on those who are housed there. Guide and protect those who have returned to the world. Grant all of them true contrition for past sins, and strengthen them in their good resolutions. Lead them along from grace to grace so that by the help of the Holy Spirit they may persevere in the ways of obedience and humility, and in the struggle against evil thoughts and desires . . . Amen

Cyprian was a leading Carthaginian lawyer, noted for his eloquence, manners and knowledge. After he was converted to Christianity in middle age, he sold off his estates and gave the proceeds to the poor. He was ordained as a priest and when the Bishop of Carthage died in AD 248 Cyprian was chosen by popular acclamation as his successor.

Soon afterwards, the Decian persecution started. Many Christians converted back to paganism, some fled, some were martyred. Cyprian himself left Carthage. He was criticized for this, but he argued that it was good military tactics; generals should not put themselves in the firing line. But after an absence of more than a year he returned before the persecutions were over. He then had to deal firmly but fairly with the Christian 'apostates', the Christians who had converted to paganism to save their lives, and who now wished to convert back again. He tried to operate a middle-way policy that was neither too lax nor too punitive.

In 257 another persecution began. Summoned before the proconsul, he declared himself a Christian and was banished. During his year-long exile, he wrote a book about Heretical Baptism. In 258, the persecution became more severe. An edict was passed ordering all bishops, priests and deacons to be executed. Cyprian was taken back to Carthage for questioning and sentenced to death. On 14 September, attended by a priest and a subdeacon, he was beheaded in front of a huge, sympathetic crowd. Even the executioner was reluctant to see Cyprian die; he was, after all, one of the leading citizens of Carthage.

Hildegard of Bingen

Chronicle

BORN

1098 at Bockelheim, Germany

DIED

1179 at Bingen

HILDEGARD'S VISIONS

And it came to pass . . . when I was 42 years and 7 months old, that the heavens were opened and a blinding light of exceptional brilliance flowed through my entire brain. And so it kindled my whole heart and breast like a flame, not burning but warming...and suddenly I understood of the meaning of expositions of the books . . .

But although I heard and saw these things, because of doubt and low opinion of myself and because of diverse sayings of men, I refused for a long time a call to write, not out of stubbornness but out of humility, until weighed down by a scourge of god, I fell onto a bed of sickness.

Hildegard was born at Bockelheim in Germany in 1098. She was educated by a recluse called Jutta and became a nun at 15. Her life was uneventful for the next 17 years. Then the visions started. In 1136 she succeeded Jutta as Abbess of Diessenberg and began writing down her visions. The resulting book, cryptically entitled *Scivias,* was approved by the Archbishop of Mainz; St Bernard later persuaded Pope Eugenius III to give his formal approval, too.

As Hildegard's name became known, her community expanded, and she moved it to larger premises near Bingen.

Like other visionaries, she felt compelled to tell secular rulers of their mistakes. She wrote letters of reproof to the likes of Henry II of England, the Emperor Frederick Barbarossa and even Pope Eugenius himself.

There were other sides to Hildegard, too. She wrote works on medicine and natural history, poems, hymns and a morality play. The medical work is remarkable, discoursing on the circulation of blood, insanity and obsession. More conventionally, she wrote the *Lives of Saints*. She was also an artist, and the illustrations for *Scivias* have been compared with the visionary paintings of William Blake. She wrote church music. It was an amazing range of achievements.

Hildegard died at the age of nearly 80. Miracles were reported, even during her lifetime and a popular cult developed soon after she died.

St Eustace

Chronicle

BORN
as Placidas

DIED
Died in 188 by being cooked to death in a bronze statue of a bull

PATRONAGE
Hunters, hunting, huntsmen, fire prevention, firefighters, Madrid, torture victims, trappers

NAME MEANING
God is gracious; gift of God

REPRESENTATION
Saint Eustace is nearly always represented with a stag and very often he is kneeling before it. He is depicted in a famous wall painting at Canterbury Cathedral and in the magnificent stained glass windows at Chartres Cathedral

Eustace is the patron saint of hunters and is most familiar in paintings as a figure meeting a stag between whose antlers hangs a crucifix. There are churches dedicated to him in Istanbul and Rome, dating from as early as the eighth century. There are also three ancient dedications to Eustace in England.

The legend of Eustace tells of a Roman general named Placidas, serving in the time of the Emperor Trajan. Placidas was out hunting one day near Tivoli when he saw a stag carrying a crucifix; the experience converted him to Christianity. Placidas changed his name, then lost both his fortune and his family through the disgrace of his conversion. He was recalled to the army, and led his troops to victory. He was later reunited with his wife and two sons, who then suffered martyrdom with him. After refusing to offer sacrifice to Roman gods, they were roasted to death in a brass bull.

It is unclear why Eustace was as popular in England as he was elsewhere in Christendom. On the west front of Wells Cathedral, he is depicted in a medieval carving carrying his children across a river.

St Matthew

Matthew, or Levi as he is called in St Mark's Gospel, was a publican or customs official in the service of King Herod. He was engaged in this work when he was called to follow Jesus. The name Matthew means 'gift of Jehovah' and it may be that his original name was Levi and he was named Matthew, perhaps by Jesus, after he accepted the call. Matthew celebrated this life-changing and momentous occasion by throwing a party. Jesus himself attended the feast, and it drew stern criticism from the Pharisees, who were scandalized that he should eat with 'publicans and sinners'. The custom was for priests and religious teachers to keep themselves apart, and Jesus conspicuously and systematically transgressed in this area, in order to show that his religion was to include everybody.

From then on, Matthew was one of the inner circle of Jesus's followers, the Apostles, who travelled everywhere with him and were in the privileged position of hearing first-hand the entire body of his teaching.

According to Eusebius, Matthew wrote his account of the ministry of Jesus out of necessity. He at first preached in Judaea and then, when he was about to travel abroad to spread the word, he wrote the story down to make up for his absence.

Matthew is said to have preached in Ethiopia and to have been a guest at one time of the eunuch of Queen Candace. According to this tradition he was eventually killed in Ethiopia. More trustworthy traditions report that he died a natural death, one of the few disciples to do so.

Chronicle

PATRONAGE

Accountants, Bankers, Bookkeepers, Custom Officials, and Tax Collectors

PRAYER

We thank thee, heavenly Father, for the witness of thine apostle and evangelist Matthew to the Gospel of thy Son our Saviour; and we pray that, after his example, we may with ready wills and hearts obey the calling of our Lord to follow him; through Jesus Christ our Lord, who liveth and reigneth with thee and the Holy Spirit, one God, now and for ever.

St Jerome

Jerome, who is sometimes known by the Latin form of his name, Hieronymus, was born in 331 near Aquileia in Dalmatia. His parents were well-off and he was educated by his father and the grammarian Donatus to become a lawyer, though he evidently did not enjoy his chosen profession. As an old man, he reminisced, 'Now that I am an old white-haired man with a bald head, I often dream I am holding forth in some petty case; when I wake up I congratulate myself that I am free from the agony of making speeches.'

Jerome pursued his law studies in Rome for some years, reading widely. His favourite author was Cicero, but he also read some theology. It was while he was in Rome that he visited churches and catacombs and was eventually baptised. After that he travelled widely, visiting Germany and the East. While he was in Antioch he fell ill and had a feverish vision in which he saw himself confronted by God on the throne of Judgement. He was asked who he was and when he answered that he was a Christian, the voice said, 'You lie. You are a Ciceronian.' As has often happened to people over the centuries, Jerome's life was threatened and uncertainty about the future forced him to start reconsidering what he was doing with his life, to take stock, to change direction. For many other saints besides Jerome, it was illness that changed their lives.

When he recovered, Jerome retired into the desert and lived as a hermit near Mavonia in Chalcis. He taught himself Hebrew, just for the self-discipline of the exercise. 'What difficulties I underwent! How often I despaired! How often I gave up and started again!' After two or three years in retreat, Jerome was ordained priest in Antioch before travelling to Constantinople and Rome.

Many Roman ladies accepted his teaching, but he was not popular, largely because he roundly criticised the manners of the Roman clergy and advocated the monastic life. This behaviour did not go down well

Chronicle

BORN
331 near Aquileia, Dalmatia

DIED
Died on 30 September, 420 at Bethlehem, following a long illness

REPRESENTATION
Reputed to have tamed a lion who became his faithful companion, St Jerome is often represented holding a crozier of a cardinal in the company of a lion

in Rome. Jerome finally left Rome in disgust in 385 with a Roman lady called Paula. They travelled together to Palestine and Egypt and settled in Bethlehem, where Jerome built a small monastery. He lived there until his death in 419. Paula established a convent nearby. It was in these final years in Jerusalem that Jerome accomplished the great work of his life, translating the Bible into Latin, and it is for this great achievement that he is now remembered. Yet Jerome wrote other works as well. He wrote biographies of Egyptian hermits and Roman women saints. He also championed the cause of monasticism and engaged in many controversial arguments; those who chose to debate with him suffered withering attacks.

He died in Bethlehem and was buried there, though his remains are said to have been moved to the church of Santa Maria Maggiori in Rome in the thirteenth century.

He is usually depicted as a lion; he was said to have made friends with a lion from whose paw he pulled a thorn.

St Remigius

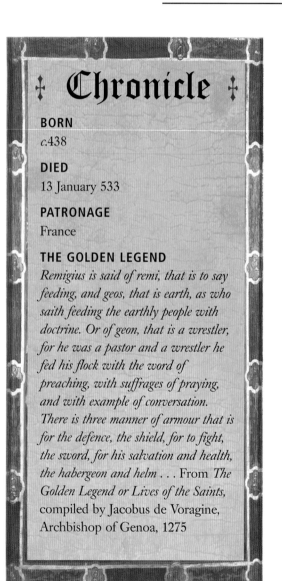

† **Chronicle** †

BORN
c.438

DIED
13 January 533

PATRONAGE
France

THE GOLDEN LEGEND
Remigius is said of remi, that is to say feeding, and geos, that is earth, as who saith feeding the earthly people with doctrine. Or of geon, that is a wrestler, for he was a pastor and a wrestler he fed his flock with the word of preaching, with suffrages of praying, and with example of conversation. There is three manner of armour that is for the defence, the shield, for to fight, the sword, for his salvation and health, the habergeon and helm . . . From *The Golden Legend or Lives of the Saints*, compiled by Jacobus de Voragine, Archbishop of Genoa, 1275

Remigius was born at Laon in France in the late fifth century, a contemporary of King Clovis. When Remigius was 21, the clergy and lay-people of Rheims gathered in the cathedral to elect a new bishop. A shaft of sunlight shone into the cathedral, lighting up the young man's face. The assembled congregation saw this and took it as a miraculous sign that God was singling him out. They accordingly chose Remigius. He was a layman and under the required age, which should have disqualified him from taking office, but they made him Archbishop of Rheims nonetheless.

When the Frankish King Clovis promised to convert to Christianity after a hard-won victory, his wife sent for Remigius to prepare Clovis for baptism and instruct him in the new faith. Converting a king was invariably a successful route to converting an entire population. When Clovis was baptized, 3,000 of his warriors were baptized with him. Archbishop Remigius stooped over the font carrying out the baptisms and he said, 'Adore what you have burnt. Burn what you have adored.'

Remigius became famous for his scholarship and eloquence. He was a very striking figure and was also immensely tall – 7 feet (2.1 metres) tall according to one account.

St Francis of Assisi

Francesco Bernadone was born in Assisi in 1181. As a young man, he was high-spirited and exceptionally well-mannered. He fought against Perugia and was taken prisoner. When he returned home he fell sick and became dissatisfied with his old way of life. At first he tried to shed these misgivings by becoming a soldier of fortune and going off to war. He became ill again and this time he decided to renounce the world.

Francis gave away all his money and travelled to Rome, where he ministered to lepers in a hospital. It was not long before he decided to lead a religious life. When he returned to Assisi he was thought mad, and children threw stones at him. He was still in a confused state of mind, but when at Mass he heard the words of the Gospel, he knew what he had to do: 'As you go, preach, saying "The kingdom of Heaven is at hand." Heal the sick, raise the dead, cleanse the lepers, cast out devils.'

Another rich man in Assisi, Bernard, was struck by the humility and meekness of Francis and joined him. Others soon followed. Francis insisted that they lived as simply as possible, owned nothing and shunned any kind of decoration. They built huts to live in, wore the coarse brown tunics of peasants, begged for food, looked after the sick. Sometimes they met at the Portiuncula, the Chapel of St Mary of the Angels, for prayer. In 1210, Francis and eleven of his brethren went to seek the Pope's approval for the 'rule' of their new order.

In 1219, Francis went to the East, where he is said to have visited the camps of both Crusaders and Saracens. Francis began a fast in August 1224 and in September he had a vision of Jesus and found afterwards that he had received the stigmata, the marks of the nails of Christ's crucifixion, in his hands and feet.

In September 1225, following a traumatic and unsuccessful eye operation, Francis returned to Assisi to die. He asked to be taken to the Portiuncula, and died on 3 October 1226, praising God to the last. A swarm of larks flocked round the roof of the house where he lay, then flew off to wheel round it in a circle. Their sweet singing seemed to be in praise of God, just as Francis had asked them. A great church was built at Assisi in his honour.

Francis is remembered as the sweetest-natured of men, and above all for his love of animals. They were all brothers and sisters to him. He would even remove Brother Worm from the path for fear he might be trodden under foot. It was said that he was seldom without a lamb for company Francis was an exceptional, life-affirming saint; he loved the world 'and all that there is in it.'

St Denis

Chronicle

BORN
c.200

ALSO KNOWN AS
Denys; Dionysius

DIED
St Denis was beheaded on a hill at Montmartre, outside Paris c.275. The site where he actually died was originally made into a small shrine. This was later developed to become the Saint Denis Basilica.

PATRONAGE
Against frenzy, against strife, France, headaches, hydrophobia, possessed people and rabies

REPRESENTATION
Usually depicted as a beheaded Bishop who is carrying his own severed head. There is usually a halo encircling the area where his head would have been

St Denis is the patron saint of France. He was sent by St Clement of Rome to preach the Gospel in Gaul. He settled in a Roman city then called Lutetia Parisiorum, only later shortened to Paris. The Parisians did not receive Denis kindly at all. In AD 258 they put him and his companions Eleutherius and Rusticus to death on a hill overlooking the city, the hill subsequently known as Montmartre, the martyr's mount.

According to one story, after the execution the body of St Denis stood up, took its head under its arm and, accompanied by an angel, walked to the site of the Abbey of St Denis. This is why he is often seen depicted as a bishop holding his head in his hands.

The great folk-hero of the French dark ages, Clovis, is said to have charged into battle shouting, 'Mon Joie Saint Denis!' meaning 'My Jove is St Denis.' This battle-cry was taken up by later medieval kings. The site of St Denis's martyrdom became the site of one of the great landmarks of Paris, the Church of the Sacred Heart, Le Sacre Coeur, Montmartre. St Genevieve buried the body of St Denis at Montmartre in 459 and built a chapel over it. King Dagobert later built the Abbey of St Denis on the same spot; for centuries this was the burial place of the Kings of France.

LINDISFARNE

æ647

ST. WILFRID

634a. d.709

St Wilfrid

Wilfrid was born into an aristocratic Northumbrian family in AD 634. He was sent to Lindisfarne for his education; there he became infected with a love of learning and the monastic life. While still a young man, he travelled to Canterbury and Rome. When he came back, he founded monasteries at Ripon and Stamford.

Wilfrid became something of a celebrity at the Synod of Whitby in AD 664, where he emerged as the champion of the Roman customs. His arguments held the day against those in favour of the British customs. After that, he was made Bishop of York. He went to France to be consecrated. While he was away, Chad was made Bishop of York in his place and Chad held the see for four years. While he was dispossessed in this way, Wilfrid founded a monastery at Oundle and acted as Bishop of Mercia, before being formally installed as Bishop of York. He held that see for nine years, during which time he founded the Abbey of Hexham.

Wilfrid managed to offend the King of Northumbria, Egfrith, who split Wilfrid's diocese into four without even telling him. Wilfrid travelled to Rome to appeal against this treatment, and the Pope upheld his appeal. But when he returned to Northumbria, he was accused of forging the Pope's seal and sent to prison.

When he was released, Wilfrid went to Sussex, then still a hotbed of paganism, to preach Christianity. When he reached Sussex, the inhabitants were suffering from a famine produced by three years of drought; people were drowning themselves out of sheer despair. He was driven out by one community, but eventually established a religious community on the island of Selsey in West Sussex.

Archbishop Theodore of Canterbury lay dying, and now wished to nominate Wilfrid as his successor, but Wilfrid refused to accept. Instead he used Theodore's good opinion of him to arrange a return to Northumbria. But when he got there things were little better than when he had left, and he was forced to withdraw to Mercia. When St Chad died, Wilfrid succeeded him as Bishop of Lichfield. A Northumbrian council attempted to recall Wilfrid in order to put him on trial; he was once again condemned and once again he appealed to Rome. This time the judgement of Rome was accepted by the bishops and nobles of Northumbria.

Wilfrid's remaining years were spent in quiet retirement at Hexham and Ripon. His final public act was to consecrate Evesham Abbey in AD 709. He died while travelling back to his monastery at Oundle and was buried at Ripon.

Wilfrid led a troubled and difficult life, and was opposed by lesser men at every turn, yet he was the most versatile and accomplished man of his time. He was a creator of buildings and institutions as well as a builder of faith. He was an energetic church builder, a great lover of learning and a musician who knew well how to create magnificent effects by using art, music, architecture and ceremony. He was a great creative artist.

Wilfrid stands out as the great defender of the rights of the Holy See. He fought all through his life for that very principle – first against Colman and the Scottish monks from Iona, and then against Theodore and his successor in the See of Canterbury. For this very reason much of Wilfrid's life was spent in exile. However, it is due to perseverence and powerful beliefs that he, above all others, established the authority of the Roman See in England. For that reason Wilfrid will always have a very high place among English saints.

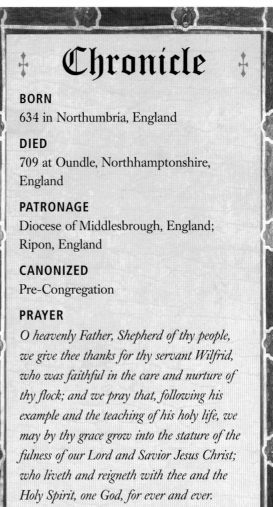

Chronicle

BORN
634 in Northumbria, England

DIED
709 at Oundle, Northhamptonshire, England

PATRONAGE
Diocese of Middlesbrough, England; Ripon, England

CANONIZED
Pre-Congregation

PRAYER
O heavenly Father, Shepherd of thy people, we give thee thanks for thy servant Wilfrid, who was faithful in the care and nurture of thy flock; and we pray that, following his example and the teaching of his holy life, we may by thy grace grow into the stature of the fulness of our Lord and Savior Jesus Christ; who liveth and reigneth with thee and the Holy Spirit, one God, for ever and ever.

Edward the Confessor

Edward the Confessor was the son of King Ethelred the Ill-Advised and Emma of Normandy. As a child he was first educated at Ely's monastery school and then, while still quite young, he was sent to Normandy – for his own safety, while Danes ruled England. In fact he lived mostly in Normandy until he became King of England in 1042. Although he was the penultimate Anglo-Saxon king, he was in his tastes and preferences a thoroughly 'Normanized' prince and not really an Anglo-Saxon king at all. French handwriting became the fashion and he preferred Norman monks to English.

Edward was temperamentally unsuited to be king. He was weak and indecisive, and preferred to spend his time hunting or in prayer. His interests were centred more in the cloister than in the court. Even so, after the Conquest by the brutal William of Normandy, many in England looked back on Edward's reign as a golden age, praying for a return to his laws. When he became king, he resolved to go on a pilgrimage to Rome, but was dissuaded by his counsellors.

He was abstemious, charitable and devout. On three occasions he watched a thief stealing from the treasury. He said nothing on the first two occasions, but on the third he warned the thief that there would be trouble if Hugolin, the treasurer, caught him. When Hugolin discovered the loss, the king tried to smooth things over by explaining that the thief needed the money more than they did. This story was told as an illustration of Edward's benevolence and charity, but it could equally well illustrate his unsuitability to rule.

It is hard now to see why Edward was regarded as saintly, though no-one disputed his canonization at the time. It may be simply that his gentleness and piety, his lack of brutality, his sheer unworldliness, were enough to mark him out as an exceptional king. He was called 'the Confessor' because he suffered for his faith, though not to the point of martyrdom; as a youth he had been compelled to go into exile for fear of the heathen Danes. Edward certainly looked saintly, with his rosy cheeks, white flowing hair and thin, translucent hands, 'in whose touch there was a kind of magic'. Often he smiled or laughed at something unseen.

Edward the Confessor's great work was the building of Westminster Abbey which was completed and dedicated just before his death in 1066. He was buried there.

Miracles were claimed at the dream-king's tomb, which became a shrine attracting many pilgrims. Westminster Abbey became associated with the idea of kingship and was from then on the chosen place for the coronation of English kings and queens.

St Etheldreda

☩ Chronicle ☩

BORN

c.640 also known as Audrey

DIED

St Etheldreda died in 679 of a large neck tumour

PATRONAGE

Cambridge University, neck ailments, throat ailments, widows

REPRESENTATION

Woman with a crown holding a staff

SAINT AUDREY'S FAIR

During the Middle Ages, there was a festival held called *Saint Audrey's Fair*. It was held on St Etheldreda's feast day in Ely. Because of the inferior quality of the merchandise at the fair, a word was added to the English language – *tawdry* – which was a corruption of 'Saint Audrey'.

Etheldreda was a seventh century East Anglian princess, daughter of King Anna. She was married twice. Her first husband, Tondbert, gave her the Isle of Ely as a dowry. He seems to have accepted her wish to spend the rest of her life in religious seclusion. After Tondbert's death her family forced her into a second marriage, this time with Egfrith, King of Northumbria. Again she expressed the wish for a celibate life and was encouraged in this by St Wilfrid. Egfrith bitterly resented it, but eventually agreed to a separation.

Etheldreda took the veil at Coldingham, but she almost immediately founded a monastery for both men and women at Ely. She was its first abbess, consecrated by St Wilfrid, then Bishop of York.

At Ely, Etheldreda lived a simple and austere life, eating only once a day, and died after being abbess for seven years. When she was dying, she suffered from an abscess on her neck, which she interpreted as a punishment for her pleasure in wearing jewellery when she was young. When her coffin was opened sixteen years after her death, her body was perfectly preserved. In the middle ages this was commonly taken to be a sign of special sanctity; the same claim was made regarding St Cuthbert's body.

Etheldreda is said to have been a woman of great beauty. She won the affections of many men – not only her two long-suffering husbands. To her friend and advisor, St Wilfred, she gave land for his abbey at Hexham, and she asked St Cuthbert on Lindisfarne to remember her in his prayers.

St Luke

Chronicle

BORN

Antioch

DIED

c.74 in Greece

PATRONAGE

Physicians and surgeons

REPRESENTATION

St Luke is often depicted with an ox or a calf because they are considered to be symbols of the sacrifice that Jesus made

PRAYER

Most charming and saintly Physician, you were animated by the heavenly Spirit of love. In faithfully detailing the humanity of Jesus, you also showed his divinity and his genuine compassion for all human beings. Inspire our physicians with your professionalism and with the divine compassion for their patients.

Luke is one of the most familiar names from the New Testament. According to Christian tradition, he was a Syrian from Antioch, a doctor by profession and neither Jewish nor a disciple of Jesus.

On Paul's second missionary journey Luke joined Paul at Troas and was then left behind at Philippi, where Paul picked him up again on the third journey. After that, Luke went with Paul to Jerusalem and Rome, where the two were imprisoned together. He is mentioned in Paul's letters to the Colossians, Philemon and Timothy. In Paul's second letter to Timothy, written not long before his execution, he said with some poignancy, 'Only Luke is with me.'

Luke's portrayal of Jesus is of a master who cares equally for women as he does for men. His account, at a time when the status of women was quite low, is consequently unique, and possibly a result of having learned much about Jesus from the Virgin Mary.

It was said that after serving Christ faultlessly Luke died in Bithynia at the age of 74.

Luke is the author of the third gospel, known as the Gospel according to St Luke, *and* the Acts of the Apostles. There are traditions that he was a painter as well as a doctor, and that he preached in Achaia, in Greece, but they are unconfirmed.

St Luke's symbol is the ox, a useful and conscientious animal – and one that is available for sacrifice, though it seems Luke was not called on to give up his life for his faith.

St Frideswide

Chronicle

ALSO KNOWN AS

Fredeswida, Fredeswinda, Frevisse, Friday, Frideswida, Fris

BORN

c.650 in the upper Thames region, England

DIED

Died of natural causes c.735

PATRONAGE

Patron and protector of Oxford and the University of Oxford, England

REPRESENTATION

She is usually depicted as a Benedictine nun

READING

Whatsoever is not God is nothing.

Frideswide was the daughter of a Mercian prince living in Oxford. She was a contemporary of St Boniface and the Venerable Bede, became a nun and founded her own convent.

She was considered a great beauty, and a neighbouring prince by the name of Algar proposed marriage. When he was rejected, he invaded Oxford with his army. Frideswide escaped from Oxford by river with two other nuns; the boat was rowed by a young man dressed in white – they assumed he was an angel – and they hid in the woods at Binsey. According to legend the prince was struck blind and his sight was only restored at her intercession.

When Frideswide returned to Oxford she cured a leper by kissing him. She settled down at her convent, devoting her time to the poor and needy, nursing the sick and teaching, eventually dying in 735. Later the convent was taken over by Augustinian canons and then acquired by Cardinal Wolsey, who turned it into Cardinal College, now known as Christ Church College. The convent chapel was rebuilt in the twelfth century to become Oxford's cathedral, and it still functions as the chapel of Christ Church College.

For centuries Frideswide's tomb was a major attraction for pilgrims. It was one of the many shrines robbed by Henry VIII, though Frideswide's bones were left in place. It was in Edward VI's reign that her remains were thrown out – to make way for the wife of Peter Martyr. Mary Tudor swapped the remains round again, then Elizabeth I ordered both women to be buried in the same grave.

St Crispin and St Crispinian

Chronicle

PATRONAGE

Cobblers, glove makers, lace makers, lace workers, leather workers, saddle makers, saddlers, shoemakers, tanners, weavers

READING

Saints Crispin and Crispinian were shoemakers; the Blessed Virgin was taken up in the care of her poor cottage; Christ himself worked with his reputed father, and those saints who renounced all commerce with the world to devote themselves totally to the contemplation of heavenly things, made mats, tilled the earth, or copied and bound good books.

The two brothers, Crispin and Crispinian, were Romans who settled modestly in Soissons in the third century. They were shoemakers by trade and also Christian missionaries. They had left Rome in an attempt to escape from the persecutions of the Emperor Diocletian. They set up their shoemakers' stall in Soissons, where they talked as they worked. They were friendly and hospitable, and welcomed anyone who wanted to come and hear about Christ while they went on making shoes.

In 287 they were denounced as Christians during a local persecution and taken before a tribunal. They were asked whether they worshipped the Roman Jupiter, Diana, Apollo, Mercury or Saturn. They replied that they worshipped the 'One-Only God'. When they were asked why they had come to Gaul, they answered that they had come 'for the love of Jesus Christ'. The place where Crispin and Crispinian were held prisoner is still marked in Soissons; it was part of the residence of the Roman governor. There they were tortured with fire but refused to recant. In the end they were both executed.

Crispin and Crispinian became the patron saints of shoemakers and models of brotherly love. The name of Crispin has become more familiar because Shakespeare included it in one of the most famous speeches he wrote, for Henry V before the Battle of Agincourt, which was fought on St Crispin's Day in 1415.

St Edmund Arrowsmith

FEAST DAY: 25 OCTOBER

Edmund Arrowsmith was born at Haydock in 1585, at a time when anti-Catholic feeling ran high in England. Both his parents, Margery and Robert, were imprisoned for their faith. Edmund wanted to study theology, and his parents thought it safer for him to do this abroad, so they sent him to the English college at Douai. He was ordained in 1612 and returned to England the next year.

Arrowsmith began preaching in Lancashire with a complete disregard for his own safety. He ministered to Catholics in Lancashire for ten years, but was then arrested and taken before the Anglican Bishop of Chester. James I was at that moment trying to arrange a Spanish marriage for his son. Severely punishing a Catholic would have been seen as an undiplomatic gesture by Catholic Spain, so Arrowsmith and other imprisoned Catholic priests were released.

It was not long before Arrowsmith was in trouble again, this time after rebuking a fellow Catholic named Holden for an allegedly incestuous marriage. In revenge Holden chose to report Arrowsmith to the authorities. In 1628, Arrowsmith was condemned as a Jesuit priest, to hanging, drawing and quartering. Beforehand, he was kept chained up for two days without food, to give him the opportunity to recant, but he refused. His last words on the day of his barbaric execution at Lancaster on 28 August 1628 were, 'Good Jesus'.

Edmund Arrowsmith was beatified in 1929 and canonized in 1970 as one of the Forty Martyrs of England and Wales. His hand is preserved at St Oswald's church in Ashton-in-Makerfield.

✝ Chronicle ✝

BORN
Originally known as Brian Arrowsmith, he was born in 1585 at Haydock, Lancashire, England

DIED
On 28 August, 1628 he was hanged, drawn and quartered at Lancaster

CANONIZED
1970 by Pope Paul VI as one of the Forty Martyrs of England and Wales

BEATIFIED
1929 by Pope Pius XI

St Edmund Campion

Chronicle

BORN
24 January, 1540 at London, England

DIED
Publicly hanged, drawn and quartered on 1 December, 1581 at Tyburn, England for treason

CANONIZED
1970 by Pope Paul VI as one of the Forty Martyrs of England and Wales

READINGS
And touching our Society, be it known to you that we have made a league – all the Jesuits in the world – cheerfully to carry the cross you shall lay upon us, and never to despair your recovery, while we have a man left to enjoy your Tyburn, or to be racked with your torments or consumed with your prisons. The expense is reckoned, the enterprise is begun; it is of God, it cannot be withstood. So the faith was planted; so it must be restored.

Excerpt from Campion's *Brag*

Born in 1540, Edmund Campion was the son of a London bookseller. He was educated at Christ's Hospital and St John's College, Oxford, where he became a Fellow. When Elizabeth I visited Oxford in 1566, it was Campion who was chosen to make the speech of welcome; he was exceptionally brilliant and – unexpectedly – exceptionally popular, too.

Campion was ordained deacon of the Church of England in 1569, but was torn by spiritual doubts. As a kind of escape, he went to Ireland to help found Trinity College, Dublin, and wrote a *History of Ireland*. He returned to England, but in about 1572 he made the momentous decision to switch to Catholicism. In 1573 he went to Rome to join the Society of Jesus. In 1579 he and Robert Persons were persuaded by Dr Allen to start a Jesuit mission in England. Campion set off for England, visiting Charles Borromeo in Milan on the way, and landed at Dover disguised as a jewel merchant.

From the moment he set foot back in England, Campion was in extreme danger. Catholics were seen by Elizabeth I's government as untrustworthy; Jesuits were seen as dangerous. Campion bravely ministered to Catholic prisoners in London and even challenged the Privy Council for the right to preach the Gospel freely. His eloquence, courage, learning and winning personality gave new heart to English Catholics. Elizabeth's government could not ignore him, but he was very mobile and very elusive. His most famous work, the *Decem Rationes*, written while he was at Stonor in Oxford-shire, was a challenge to Protestants to debate with him the foundations of the Catholic faith. Four hundred copies of this book were secretly distributed before the Commemoration Service at St Mary's Church in Oxford. A few weeks later he was arrested at Lyford Grange in Berkshire and imprisoned in the Tower of London.

He was interrogated, cajoled and tortured, but nothing would make him recant. They even tried to bribe him, to no avail. In November 1581, he was put on trial in Westminster Hall on a trumped-up charge of plotting rebellion. Campion defended himself ably, but the result of the trial was inevitable. Sentenced to a horrible death he said, 'In condemning us, you condemn all your own ancestors, all the ancient bishops and kings, all that was once the glory of England.' He died at Tyburn on 1 December 1581, along with Alexander Briant and Ralph

Sherwin. They were publicly hanged, drawn and quartered, an appalling death that was the standard punishment for treason in England in those times. A great patriot was needlessly lost that day: he remained intensely loyal to the Queen he had welcomed to Oxford long before. He was also a great literary stylist who would have gone on to write books to equal those of any of his Elizabethan contemporaries. Above all, England lost a brilliant, charismatic and immensely likeable personality. Edmund Campion was canonized in 1970 as one of the Forty Martyrs of England and Wales.

St Margaret Clitherow

✝ Chronicle ✝

BORN

1556 as Margaret Middleton at York, England

DIED

Death by *peine forte et dure*, which literally means she was pressed to death on Good Friday, 25 March, 1586 at Tyburn, York, England

PATRONAGE

Businesswomen, converts, martyrs

CANONIZED

1970 by Pope Paul VI

READINGS

Saint Margaret, when asked to confess her crimes before execution said,

I die for the love of my Lord Jesu.

and her last words were:

Jesu! Jesu! Jesu! Have mercy on me.

Margaret was born in York in 1556, the daughter of a candle-maker called Thomas Middleton. She was brought up as a Protestant, marrying John Clitherow, a wealthy Protestant butcher in 1571. Three years later she became a convert to Catholicism, though her husband remained a staunch Protestant. They remained on good terms, though John was obliged to pay regular fines for his wife's absence from Anglican church services.

Margaret Clitherow became more outspoken as time passed, and this led to a two-year spell in prison. She used this time to learn to read and on her release she set up a dame school, teaching her own and her neighbours' children. This was a dangerous course of action, yet John allowed her to follow her own destiny, even when it involved giving shelter to fugitive priests in a specially-built priest-hole.

In 1586, John was called to explain in court where his missing son was; in fact the boy was studying at a Catholic college on the European mainland. The authorities were suspicious, searched the Clitherow house for evidence of Catholic activity and found nothing. Then they interrogated the children, and one of them revealed the whereabouts of the secret room. There they found the damning evidence – vessels and vestments for the Catholic Mass. Margaret was arrested and brought to trial.

For fear of incriminating her friends, Margaret refused to say anything. She was sentenced to death and on 25 March 1586 she was pressed to death beneath an 800-pound weight. The terrible death she suffered led to the immediate development of a cult following.

St Carlo (Charles) Borromeo

✠ Chronicle ✠

BORN

Wednesday, 2 October, 1538 in the castle at Aron, diocese of Novara, Italy

DIED

3 November, 1584 of a fever at Milan, Italy

PATRONAGE

Against ulcers, apple orchards, bishops and stomach diseases

PRAYER

O Saintly reformer, animator of spiritual renewal of priests and religious, you organized true seminaries and wrote a standard catechism. Inspire all religious teachers and authors of catechetical books. Move them to love and transmit only that which can form true followers of the Teacher who was divine. Amen.

Carlo, the son of Count Gilbert Borromeo, was born in 1538 at the family's ancestral castle on Lake Maggiore. He was educated at Paris and Milan, where he proved a devout, diligent and intelligent student. At the early age of 22, in spite of his speech impediment, he was appointed secretary of state, administrator of Milan and cardinal; these surprisingly premature advancements came about because of an invaluable family connection – his uncle was Pope Pius IV.

Borromeo moved to Rome, where he acted as the Pope's legate. He was now a grandee, and he kept a lavish household to match his high status, but this ostentation worried him. He even considered resigning to become a monk.

He was responsible for many of the reforms passed at the Council of Trent. In 1563, he became Bishop of Milan, which he found was in desperate need of all the reforms he had advocated at Trent. He set about raising moral and educational standards in the clergy. He adopted a humbler lifestyle than before, distributing his wealth to the poor. When famine struck in 1570, and then plague in 1576, Carlo Borromeo was heavily involved in organising and carrying out the relief work.

He worked tirelessly for the people of Milan and died, worn out at the age of 46, in 1584. A popular cult sprang up immediately and he was canonized in 1610. His reforming zeal made him bitter enemies, but he was greatly loved by the ordinary people he helped.

St Leo the Great

✦ Chronicle ✦

BORN

c.400 at Tuscany, Italy

DIED

11 April, 461 at Rome, Italy and his relics are preserved in the Vatican basilica

PATRONAGE

Choristers and musicians

READING

Dear friends, now that we have received instruction in this revelation of God's grace, let us celebrate with spiritual joy the day of our first harvesting, of the first calling of the Gentiles. Let us give thanks to the merciful God, "who has made us worthy," in the words of the Apostle, "to share the position of the saints in light; who has rescued us from the power of darkness, and brought us into the kingdom of this beloved Son."
From a sermon by Leo the Great

Leo became pope in 449, at a time when the Western Empire was breaking up and there were many diverging views about the Christian faith. As a theologian, Leo held the view that Jesus had been in the fullest sense a human being. This was under attack by the Manichaeans, who believed that matter itself was evil, and that therefore God could never have come to earth 'in the flesh'.

There was a Council at Ephesus, at which the views of the Manichaeans and others who thought similarly, such as Eutyches, were pronounced orthodox. Leo was represented at the council by legates, but they were overridden. The Church did not accept the verdict of the Robber Council, as many there were voting under pressure. In 451, at the Council of Chalcedon, a treatise by Leo on the Incarnation (Jesus as God made flesh) was read – and acclaimed. It was a turning-point in Christian history.

Leo also played a role in history outside the Church. When Attila the Hun invaded and conquered Italy with his hordes, Leo confronted Attila in his pontifical robes and persuaded him to withdraw. Leo tried this again when Genseric the Vandal arrived at the walls of Rome. Leo met Genseric to urge him not to destroy the city. This time he was unsuccessful, and Rome was sacked, but Leo even so had shown remarkable courage.

He was a strict and uncompromising pope, but the times demanded strength and resolution. Leo's defence of the idea of Jesus as a man was a historic landmark in the development of Christianity.

LEO MAGNVS

St Martin

Martin was born of pagan parents in Pannonia (modern Austria) in the fourth century. Although he wanted to be both a Christian and a monk, at fifteen his father made him join the army. While he was stationed at Ambianum, near Amiens, Martin was riding one wintry day by the city gate when he saw a naked beggar asking for alms. Martin cut his cloak in two with his sword and gave the beggar half of it. His companion ridiculed the gesture, but that night Martin had a dream in which he saw Christ surrounded by angels – and wearing the half-cloak he had given to the beggar. After the dream, Martin was baptized without delay.

After he had served for five years in the army, and the German war was over, Martin asked to be released from active service. He was taunted with the charge of cowardice and put in irons, though later released.

Martin went to Bishop Hilary of Poitiers for instruction, and later founded a monastery there. He became Bishop of Tours, and was visited by so many people that he withdrew to a cave in a cliff above the River Loire. He was followed by eighty disciples, who hollowed cave dwellings for themselves out of the sandstone. The local people were mostly pagan, and Martin's work was mainly preaching and conversion. He made it his business to pull down pagan temples and replace them with churches and chapels.

On one occasion, when Count Avitianus arrived at Tours bringing with him a crowd of captives for execution, Martin went to Avitianus's house and stretched himself out on the doorstep in silent prayer, hoping that the captives' lives would be spared. Avitianus found him and said, 'I know what you have come to ask. I grant their lives and liberty at your unspoken prayer.' Later Martin interceded with the Emperor Maximus to spare the lives of Priscillian and six other Christians, but was unsuccessful; they were beheaded. Martin was extremely angry, especially with the bishops who had connived at these executions. For a long time he refused to communicate with them, and then it was only after an assurance from Maximus that he would persecute no more followers of Priscillian.

Martin himself survived to the age of eighty, dying on 9 November AD 401 at Candes. He was buried at Tours, attended by two thousand monks. It was said that the boat bearing his body floated upstream, to the sound of heavenly music, without sail or oars; the trees on the river bank burst into flower.

St Edmund Rich

Chronicle

BORN

November *c*.1170 at Abingdon, Berkshire, England

DIED

He died of natural causes *c*.1242 at the Cistercian monastery in Pontigny, Burgundy, France

PATRONAGE

Abingdon, England, diocese of Portsmouth, England

REPRESENTATION

Although St Edmund Rich is often depicted placing a ring on the finger of a statue of the Blessed Virgin Mary or embracing the child Jesus, in the picture on the opposite page we see him holding a staff and reading the bible

Edmund Rich was born at Abingdon probably in 1170, which was the momentous year when Thomas Becket was martyred at Canterbury. Edmund, too, was to become Archbishop of Canterbury, though he did not take the risks Thomas took. His parents were devout Christians, but his father died while Edmund was still a boy. Edmund studied in Paris, then returned to lecture in the Arts at Oxford for six years. Thereafter he returned to Paris to study theology.

Edmund was ordained as a priest and led a life of extreme austerity, sleeping on a bare floor and wearing a hair shirt. In 1222 he returned to England to become Treasurer at Salisbury Cathedral. He became famous as a preacher, preaching a crusade at several cities, including Oxford, Worcester and Gloucester. In 1233 he was elected Archbishop of Canterbury and in that role he offered steady though ineffectual opposition to Henry III and the excessive exactions of tax from the Pope. He supported the council in their move to have the king's foreign counsellors dismissed.

Ultimately he seems to have given up in despair, withdrawing to Pontigny, where he spent his time in prayer. He died at Soissy in 1242 and was buried at Pontigny, where his shrine still stands behind the high altar. In spite of protests from Henry III, Archbishop Edmund Rich was canonized in 1246. The archbishop was the founder of St Edmund Hall, the last of Oxford's medieval colleges.

St Hilda

Chronicle

BORN

614 at Northumbria, England

DIED

Having suffered from illness for the last six years of her life, St Hilda died of natural causes on 17 November, 680

REPRESENTATION

Often represented holding Whitby Abbey in her hands with a crown on her head or at her feet or, as seen on the opposite page, holding the Bible and a staff

PRAYER

O God, whose blessed Son became poor that we through his poverty might be rich: deliver us from an inordinate love of this world, that, following the example of thy servant Hilda, we may serve thee with singleness of heart . . .

Hilda's father, a nobleman, was murdered when she was very young, and she was brought up at the court of King Edwin of Northumbria, her great-uncle. There she fell under the influence of the missionary Paulinus and in 627 when she was thirteen years old she was baptized at York.

Hilda was destined for the religious life and she intended to enter a convent in France, but Aidan persuaded her to stay in Northumbria. He gave her a small convent on the River Wear to tend, and then she was made abbess of the monastery at Hartlepool. She was often visited there and advised by Aidan. Then in 657 she founded her own mixed, or 'double', monastery at Whitby, which quickly became celebrated as a great seat of learning as well as a great spiritual centre.

Hilda was a great champion of the British church services when they were debated at the crucial Synod of Whitby, held at her monastery in 663–4. The ruling of the synod went against her wishes, but she accepted it. The synod marked the end of the British Church.

She was a great patron of learning, and it was not by chance that five of her monks became bishops. She acquired a reputation for wisdom, and kings and princes sought her advice. She eventually died at the age of 66 in 680. On the night when she died, a nun at Harkness, thirteen miles from Whitby, saw the top of the house open and a strange light coming out of it; it was the soul of Hilda ascending to Heaven with a company of angels.

St Hugh of Avalon

Hugh was born in about 1135, of a noble Burgundian family. His father was the lord of the Castle of Avalon near Grenoble and when Hugh's mother died his father retreated to the monastery of Villarbenoit. He took the eight-year-old Hugh with him and brought him up as a monk, the boy was never allowed to play children's games.

The English King Henry II heard about Hugh when he was at the Grande Chartreuse monastery and appointed him Prior of a Carthusian house at Witham in Somerset, founded as a penance for the murder of Becket. The King held Hugh in high regard; Hugh was one of the few men to whom he would listen. Hugh eventually became Bishop of Lincoln. When Hugh dared to excommunicate the head forester, the King was furious and summoned him to explain himself, but Hugh was able to deflate the King's terrible rage. He had a similar relationship with Henry's successor, Richard I. He refused to oblige Richard with levies of men from Lincoln for military service on the grounds that the King wanted to deploy the men overseas. Hugh travelled to Normandy to protest to the King in person. When the King ignored him, Hugh said, 'You ought to kiss me: I have come a long way to see you.' He was uncompromising, yet gentle.

He had a difficult relationship with King John, too. John began by declaring his good intentions, but Hugh said, 'You know I hate lies.' When Hugh pointedly preached a very long Easter sermon on the duties of kings, John sent word to him three times to bring it to a close, but Hugh took no notice whatever.

Hugh oversaw the building of Lincoln Cathedral and spent a great deal of time ensuring that vacant posts were filled with the right candidates.

He remained simple in his tastes and disliked displays of status. He liked to attend to all the pastoral duties of priests. He had a particular obsession with taking funerals; he saw it as an opportunity to look after the distressed.

On his deathbed in Westminster, Hugh was visited by Archbishop Hubert, who suggested that he should ask forgiveness for provoking him so much, but Hugh said he would rather ask for forgiveness for not having provoked him more. He died on a cross of ashes on the floor on 16 November 1200. He was taken from London for burial in Lincoln Cathedral. The body was met outside Lincoln by the Kings of Scotland and England and the biggest gathering of bishops and abbots ever seen. King John helped carry the coffin. St Hugh's body has never been disturbed and still rests in its coffin under the Angel Choir.

St Elizabeth
of Hungary

Elizabeth was born in 1207 at Saros in Hungary, the daughter of King Andrew II of Hungary. At the age of four she was sent to live at the court of the Landgrave of Thuringia, as it was already decided that she should marry the Landgrave's son Louis. When the two married only 10 years later, it proved to be a love match and they were very happy, living at the Wartburg castle near Eisenach.

Elizabeth was now in a position to give full rein to her impulsive and generous nature. She threw herself into the task of building hospitals, giving money to the poor and offering care to orphans. This idyllically happy period came to an abrupt end when news came that her husband had died of plague at Otranto while on Crusade. Elizabeth was overwhelmed with grief. Then her brother-in-law evicted her from the Wartburg, claiming that she had mismanaged and squandered Louis's estate. She had promised Louis that she would never marry again and, after making provision for her children, she entered a Franciscan religious house at Marburg in Hesse, devoting the rest of her life to helping the poor and needy.

She worked tirelessly, driven on by her sadistic spiritual adviser, Conrad of Marburg. He cruelly made her dismiss her two ladies-in-waiting, friends since childhood, and frequently gave her beatings. The combination of unrelenting work, deprivation, grief and physical abuse led to her death at the age of 24. She was canonized soon afterwards and her shrine at Marburg became a popular destination for pilgrims.

✝ Chronicle ✝

BORN
1207 at Saros, Hungary

DIED
17 November, 1231 at Marburg at the age of 24. Her relics are preserved at the convent of Saint Elizabeth in Vienna, Austria

PATRONAGE
Patron saint of bakers, countesses, death of children, falsely accused, the homeless and nursing services

HER SYMBOLS
Alms, flowers, bread, the poor and a pitcher

St Edmund
King and Martyr

FEAST DAY: 20 NOVEMBER

Born in about 841, Edmund had the misfortune to be the last Anglo-Saxon king of East Anglia. Edmund was a Kentish (and therefore probably Jutish), prince who was appointed by King Offa of East Anglia to be his successor. Offa abdicated, like several Dark Ages kings before him, and took himself off on a pilgrimage to Rome. Edmund sailed from Kent in 855 and was crowned by Bishop Humbert on Christmas Day at Sudbury, a royal country house on the River Stour.

As a devout and conscientious Christian, Edmund departed on a year-long retreat in a tower he had built on the Norfolk coast not far from Hunstanton, at a place that is still known as St Edmund's Point.

Chronicle

BORN
c.841 probably at
Nuremburg, Germany

DIED
Martyred in Hoxne, Suffolk,
England on 20 November,
870 by the Danes

PATRONAGE
Diocese of East Anglia,
kings, plague epidemics,
torture victims, wolves

There he is said to have learnt the Psalter by heart. The people of East Anglia lived in peace and prosperity under their well-loved king until 865, when a great Danish invasion army led by Hingmar and Hubba, the sons of Ragnar Lodbrog, descended upon East Anglia. The Danes destroyed the great Fenland abbeys of Crowland, Bardney, Peterborough, Huntingdon and Ely. From the Fens the Danes advanced on Suffolk, where they set fire to the town of Thetford. There Edmund mustered his East Anglian army, but he was defeated in battle by the Danes at a place called Haegelisdun (probably Hellesdon).

After the battle, in 870, Edmund withdrew to his castle at Framlingham in the hope of preventing further, senseless slaughter. The Danes seem to have held some respect for Edmund, as they tried to find a way to spare him. He was called to parley by the Danes, who offered him peace in return for half of his wealth and his homage as a vassal prince.

Edmund was ready to give the Danes half of his treasure, but refused to become a vassal prince, unless his overlord would agree to become a Christian. His would-be master, the Danish prince Hingmar, was furious at this insulting suggestion, expecting rather that Edmund would renounce Christianity out of respect for his master. He ordered that Edmund should be whipped. He then had the East Anglian king tied to a tree and shot at by Danish archers. Edmund died full of arrows.

The martyrdom of St Edmund is said to have taken place at Hoxne. After Edmund's death, his body was unceremoniously thrown down among the trees. According to legend, the body was later found only with the help of a grey wolf. A small wooden oratory was built over the place where the body was buried. A miracle cult quickly developed at Hoxne.

In 903, thirty years after the king's murder, his incorrupt body was transferred to the new monastery of St Edmund's Bury at Beodoricesworth, later known as Bury St Edmunds, where he was given a magnificent shrine. St Edmund belongs to a small and select group of saints who were also kings. He became the patron saint of England until the adoption of the non-English St George. St Edmund's shrine became one of the great pilgrimage centres; even the great King Canute came, wearing his crown and bearing gifts for Edmund's shrine.

St Cecilia

Chronicle

BORN
Not documented

DIED
Beheaded c.117 because of her Christian beliefs

PATRONAGE
Patron saint of music and the blind

REPRESENTATION
Lute, organ, roses

PRAYER
Dear Saint Cecilia, one thing we know for certain about you is that you became a heroic martyr in fidelity to your divine Bridegroom . . . gladden the hearts of people by filling the air with God's gift of music and reminding them of the divine Musician who created all beauty. Amen

Cecilia was married to a youth called Valerian, but had nevertheless vowed to keep her virginity. In the middle ages such extreme chastity was seen as extreme virtue. When Cecilia told her husband that her virginity was under the protection of an angel, he asked her to, 'Show me the angel'. She replied that if he would convert to Christianity then he would indeed see the angel.

When he returned from his baptism by the Pope, Valerian saw Cecilia kneeling with the angel at her side holding two crowns made of roses and lilies. The angel placed the crowns on their heads and vanished.

Around the year AD 230, Cecilia was executed for being a Christian. First they tried to suffocate her in the baths, but she survived. Then they tried to behead her, but the headsman was unable to sever her head. He was only permitted three strokes, and after that her head was still not completely severed. She lingered on in this pitiful state for three days before dying. In St Cecilia's Church in Rome there is a chapel standing on the site of the baths where she was killed.

Later, Cecilia was adopted as the patron saint of music and musicians. This was because Pope Paschal I, who had her remains reburied with great ceremony in 817, gave an endowment to the monks of the monastery next to St Cecilia's Church so that they could sing without ceasing at her tomb.

St Clement

Chronicle

BORN
Rome, Italy

DIED
Martyred 101 during the persecution of Trajan

PATRONAGE
Boatmen, marble workers, mariners, sailors, sick children, stonecutters, watermen

PAPAL ASCENSION
c.88

READING
Charity unites us to God. There is nothing mean in charity, nothing arrogant. Charity knows no schism, does not rebel, does all things in concord. In charity all the elect of God have been made perfect.

Clement was the fourth Bishop of Rome after St Peter, Linus and Cletus. He is said to have been ordained as a priest by St Peter himself.

St Clement's main claim to fame is as the author of the *First Epistle of Clement to the Corinthians.*

The identity of Clement is uncertain. Some believe that he was the Clement who was the disciple who travelled and worked alongside St Paul, but others think that he may have been the Flavius Clemens who was a consul and a relation of the Emperor Domitian. This Flavius Clemens, the pagan Roman writer Suetonius tells us, was put to death on a charge of 'atheism' by Domitian, and his wife Domitilla was banished to an island in the Mediterranean. Being members of the imperial family did not save them. Domitilla owned the Domitillan Cemetery, which was a second century Christian catacomb. Flavius Clemens was perhaps brought up as a conventional Roman pagan, and converted to Christianity in middle age. Given his social status, he would have mixed with such literary figures as Juvenal and Tacitus, which might explain the literary quality of his writing.

Clement is said to have been killed by being thrown into the sea tied to an anchor. An entire 'Clementine' literature grew up based on speculation about his life. Gregory of Tours, writing in the sixth century, even describes Clement's death in the Crimea, of all places. Clement's importance rests in the way he represents a phase in the development of the early Church.

St Catherine
of Alexandria

✠ Chronicle ✠

BORN
Not documented

DIED
Beheaded c.307 in Alexandria, Egypt

REPRESENTATION
She is often portrayed carrying a spiked wheel which is supposed to depict the way in which she was to be put to death had the wheel not broken into many fragments. The firework the 'Catherine Wheel' was named after her.

PATRONAGE
Patron saint of preachers, philosophers, librarians, young girls, and craftsmen working with a wheel, e.g. potters and spinners

St Catherine is remembered for the role of the wheel in her martyrdom. She lived at the end of the third century AD in the city of Alexandria in Egypt. She was, according to later legend, young, beautiful, rich and scholarly. She attracted the attention of the Emperor Maximian, whose advances she rejected. In the year 307, Maximian confronted her with an assembly of fifty philosophers in an effort to overcome her resistance, but she was able to defeat them all in argument.

In a rage at being thwarted, Maximian ordered her to be broken on a wheel studded with spikes. The wheel was struck by 'fire from heaven' and shattered. Catherine was uninjured, but after this she was whipped and beheaded. Legend had it that her body was carried away by angels and buried on Mount Sinai.

For hundreds of years Catherine's popularity was widespread. Her reputation was carried from the eastern Mediterranean westwards to England by returning crusaders. At least eighty churches in England were dedicated to St Catherine. Her adoration rested simply on her symbolic value. She was a symbol of intelligent and resolute chastity, the beautiful but virtuous young woman who refused the advances of men. In the middle ages she was held up to both daughters and wives as the model of sexual virtue.

St Andrew

Chronicle

BORN

Bethsaida

DIED

Martyred in 70AD by being crucified on a Saltire Cross (an X-shaped cross) in Patras, Greece

PATRONAGE

Anglers, fish dealers, fish mongers, fishermen, gout, maidens, old maids, Greece, Russia, Scotland and stiff necks

PRAYER

O Glorious Saint Andrew, you were the first to recognise and follow the Lamb of God. With your friend Saint John you remained with Jesus for that first day, for your entire life, and now throughout eternity. As you led your brother Saint Peter to Christ and many others after him, draw us also to him.

Andrew was a disciple of John the Baptist before becoming the first apostle to be called by Jesus. He was a Galilean and the brother of Simon Peter; in fact Andrew's first and most significant act as Jesus's follower was to look for his brother and bring him to Jesus.

Andrew was present throughout the ministry of Jesus and played an important part in it. At the feeding of the five thousand, it was Andrew who told Jesus about the boy who had brought with him the loaves and fishes.

It is the Gospel of St John in particular that tells us of Andrew's contribution to the ministry of Jesus. Later traditions record that Andrew went on to preach to the Scythians or Greeks. In Greece he was so successful that at Patras he attracted the attention of the Roman proconsul, who ordered his execution. He had Andrew *tied* to a cross, not nailed, so that he would die more slowly. He is said to have lingered on the cross for two days before dying.

St Andrew's body was later taken by Constantine to Constantinople. St Regulus, who was in charge of Andrew's remains, was told by an angel in a dream to take them to a particular place; the angel would guide him. Regulus eventually arrived in Scotland, and the chosen spot was later known as St Andrews. Regulus was helped by King Angus MacFergus, by tradition the founder of the town of St Andrews. It was in this way that Jesus's disciple became the patron saint of Scotland.

St Berin

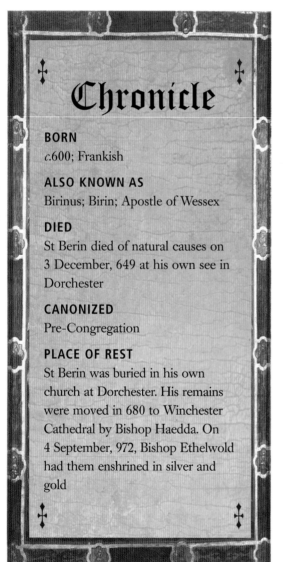

Chronicle

BORN
c.600; Frankish

ALSO KNOWN AS
Birinus; Birin; Apostle of Wessex

DIED
St Berin died of natural causes on 3 December, 649 at his own see in Dorchester

CANONIZED
Pre-Congregation

PLACE OF REST
St Berin was buried in his own church at Dorchester. His remains were moved in 680 to Winchester Cathedral by Bishop Haedda. On 4 September, 972, Bishop Ethelwold had them enshrined in silver and gold

Although firmly associated with the conversion of the southern English, Berin was a north Italian by birth, probably a Lombard. Berin's name is sometimes given as Birin, sometimes in its Latinized form, Birinus. He was consecrated as a bishop by Astorius, the Bishop of Milan, just before he set sail for Britain from Genoa in 633. The missionary voyage to Britain was approved by Pope Honorius, and the intention was to preach Christianity in those parts of the island that had not yet been converted.

Berin made his landfall in the kingdom of the West Saxons near Southampton and he found the people he encountered there so pagan that he thought he should preach to them instead of travelling any further. With this in mind he travelled inland, through what is now Hampshire, in search of the West Saxon king, Cynegils. Tradition has it that Berin first preached to Cynegils on a hill called Churn Knob near Wallingford.

Cynegils was baptized soon after this, with King Oswald of Northumbria standing as his sponsor. Oswald had come south to seek Cynegils's daughter in marriage. The two kings established Berin at Dorchester, where he built a cathedral. After that, little is known of Berin's work as Bishop of the West Saxons. His see of Dorchester became the parent of nearly all the dioceses of southern and central England.

Berin died at Dorchester on 3 December, 649. His body was later moved to Winchester by Bishop Haedda when the West Saxon see became centred there.

Francis Xavier

Chronicle

BORN

1506 in the family castle of Xavier, near Pamplona in the Basque region of Spain

DIED

2 December, 1552 of a fever on board *Santa Cruce*

BEATIFIED

25 Oct, 1619 by Pope Paul V

CANONIZED

12 March, 1622 by Pope Gregory XV

PRAYER

O God, Who didst vouchsafe, by the preaching and miracles of Saint Francis Xavier, to join unto Thy Church the nations of the Indies, grant, we beseech Thee, that we who reverence his glorious merits may also imitate his example, through Jesus Christ Our Lord

Francis Xavier was the youngest son of a nobleman of Navarre, Juan de Jasso, and born in 1506. Francis took the name Xavier from his mother. At the age of seventeen he went to the University of Paris, graduating in 1530, after which he lectured in Logic and Metaphysics. Among those attending his lectures was Ignatius Loyola, who set out to make friends with him. At first Francis was suspicious and cool, but eventually his trust was won and Francis became one of the six companions who took vows at Montmartre and so became the first Jesuits.

After spending some time in Italy, Francis was instructed by Ignatius to go with Simon Rodriguez on a mission to the East Indies. He sailed from Lisbon on 17 April 1541, the day that Ignatius was elected the first General of the Society of Jesus. There were over 900 other people on board, and conditions were not good, but Francis talked freely with the other passengers and the crew, as was always his practice. He mended quarrels, heard confessions and preached a Sunday sermon on deck. This voyage lasted over a year, including a six-month stay in Mozambique.

Francis landed at Goa in May 1542, where he began his mission in the East. His practice was to stay a few weeks in each place, teaching the children, translating some hymns and prayers into the native language, and training a native teacher to carry on when he left. He had a great gift for languages. Later, either he or another Jesuit father would revisit. His influence and power as a teacher were remarkable; he had an engaging and charming manner. He also led a life of extreme austerity.

While in the Indies, he decided to visit Japan, and sailed from Malacca in a small Chinese junk. He stayed in Japan for about two years, in spite of considerable hostility. He was once almost stoned to death. He was shouted at: 'There goes the man who tells us we must only have one wife!' Christian missionaries in Japan were severely persecuted, but Francis survived, setting off on his return voyage to Goa in 1551, where he arrived the following year, his hair having turned white.

Next he decided on a missionary journey to China, though he was obstructed this time by Portuguese officials. He had an ambitious plan to make a formal embassy to the Emperor of China; through this he hoped to negotiate a treaty between China and Portugal that would give him a platform for a Christian mission in China. Eventually he reached the island of San Chan, still over 100 miles from Canton. He was forbidden entry into Canton for three months. While he was waiting for an opportunity to sail, he was overtaken by a fever and died on board the *Santa Cruce* on 2 December 1552. Francis Xavier is remembered as one of the great pioneer Christian missionaries, ranking alongside Patrick, Boniface and Columba. He is also remembered as one of the first Jesuits. He was canonized in 1622.

St Nicholas

St Nicholas was born in Lycia (now south-west Turkey) and was Bishop of Myra in the fourth century. The Emperor Justinian dedicated a church to him in 560 and from the tenth century onwards St Nicholas was one of the most revered saints throughout the West.

Nicholas was a wealthy man and he devoted his resources to relieving the poor in the city of Myra. One of the many stories told about Nicholas, illustrating his kindness and charitable work, is that he heard about a distressed nobleman who was out of financial necessity about to condemn his three daughters to a life of prostitution. To save the girls from this disgrace, Nicholas threw a bag of gold through the nobleman's window from the street on three successive nights, giving rise to the emblem associated with St Nicholas, three golden balls, which was later to be adopted by pawnbrokers.

On a voyage to the Holy Land he saved the ship from being wrecked with his prayers, which is how he became the patron saint of travellers, sailors and those overtaken by sudden danger. He is even better known as the patron saint and protector of children. This association arose from another legendary story. During a famine, he became aware that three of his pupils were missing. He searched and eventually found their bodies at an inn, where they had been killed, cut up and pickled in a tub, ready to eat. Nicholas miraculously brought the three boys back to life.

He saved the city of Myra from famine. Some corn ships docked at Myra on their way to the port of Alexandria and Bishop Nicholas persuaded the captains of these ships to unload part of their cargo. He managed to do this by promising that when they reached Alexandria they would not be in trouble because none of the cargo would be missing. Nicholas performed a miracle and kept his promise. He also saved three innocent travellers who were unjustly condemned to death, by visiting the Emperor in a dream and persuading him to set them free.

Nicholas died in 326 and was probably buried in Myra. His body was taken for reburial at Bari in Italy in 1084.

The Feast of St Nicholas in December has become associated with Advent. St Nicholas himself, as Santa Claus, has become a central figure in the Christmas festival, benign, avuncular and caring for children.

Ο ΑΓΙΟΣ ΝΙΚΟΛΑΟΣ

St Ambrose

Along with Jerome and Augustine, Ambrose was one of the great figures of the early Church. He was born in 339, the son of Ambrosius, Praetorian Prefect of the Gauls. Ambrosius brought up his children, Ambrose and his older siblings Marcellina and Satyrus, as Christians; all three were to become saints. As a boy Ambrose was inseparable from his brother Satyrus, whether studying or walking. They went for long walks in the hills, sunk in discussion. In later years, when reading alone, Ambrose would often look up and begin to speak: he had become so used to sharing his thoughts with his brother.

Ambrose was made governor of Emilia and Liguria in northern Italy, which meant moving to Milan, then the residence of the Roman emperors and a great metropolitan centre. He found the city disturbed by religious controversy. During one riot in the basilica in 375, Ambrose arrived to restore order. As he went in, a child's voice was heard to say, 'Ambrose is bishop.' The call was taken up and Ambrose found himself appointed by acclamation, even though he had yet to be baptised. He received a letter of congratulation from St Basil of Caesarea.

Three years later, Ambrose lost his brother. Satyrus was traumatised by being shipwrecked on a voyage to Africa, and died not long after his return. In his valediction over his brother's bier, Ambrose said, 'What will become of me, my brother? The ox misses his yoke-fellow. How can I forget you? I see you at every moment, I speak to you, I press you in my arms day and night. I used to dread sleep because it interrupted our communion; now I love it, because in it I find you again.'

The life of Ambrose as a bishop was difficult and challenging. He fought ceaselessly to put right what he saw as wrongs. He was praised for winning a battle against paganism, regarding the altar to Victory in the Senate. He won a battle against the tyranny of the Emperor Theodosius. These victories gave him the highest status in the Christian community – after the martyrs. Today, some of his battles seem less worthwhile. The altar of the goddess Victory had more than once been removed from the Senate House, then put back again. To the Romans it meant more than a representation of a goddess and an 'embassy' for the gods of Olympus; it stood for patriotism, fidelity to the past. Ironically, it was Ambrose's old friend Symmachus who made a great speech defending the presence of Victory in the Senate House. But Ambrose prevailed, and the last political symbol of paganism was removed.

Ambrose confronted Theodosius with more reason. One of the emperor's officials had been murdered in Thessalonica. Theodosius decided that the city as a whole should be punished. The citizens were invited to the arena to see the games, and once inside they were massacred in their thousands. It was unjust and cruel. Ambrose refused to enter the imperial palace after that, and more daringly refused to admit the emperor into the church until he had made a public admission of his great sin. Yet Ambrose addressed Theodosius gently and warmly, made it possible for the emperor to climb down without losing face. There was a period of reflection, then a face-to-face confrontation at the door of the basilica, after which Theodosius, an intensely emotional man, went back to his palace in tears. It took eight months for Theodosius to admit publicly that he had done wrong. The confrontation, which could easily have ended in Ambrose's death, led to a friendship between the two men that lasted the rest of their lives. After the death of Theodosius, Ambrose himself had only two more years to live, dying at 57 on Easter Eve 397.

Chronicle

BORN
339 in Trier, southern Gaul (modern Germany)

DIED
St Ambrose died of natural causes on Holy Saturday, 4 April, 397 in Milan, Italy

PATRONAGE
Patron saint of beekeepers (due to the fact that a swarm of bees allegedly landed on his mouth when he was a baby), farm animals and candle makers

CANONIZED
Pre-Congregation

PRAYER
Lord Jesus Christ, I approach your banquet table in fear and trembling, for I am a sinner, and dare not rely on my own worth but only on your goodness and mercy. I am defiled by many sins in body and soul, and by my unguarded thoughts and words.

St Lucy

✝ Chronicle ✝

BORN

c.283 at Syracuse, Sicily

DIED

St Lucy died c.304 at Syracuse, Sicily; after being tortured she was stabbed to death with a dagger

PATRONAGE

Patron saint of the blind, authors, dysentery, epidemics, martyrs, peasants, Perugia, Italy, salesmen, stained glass windows, Syracuse, Italy and throat infections

PRAYER

Relying on Your goodness, O God, we humbly ask you, in the intercession of your servant, Saint Lucy, to give perfect vision to our eyes, that we may serve for your greater honour and glory.

Saint Lucy, hear our prayers and obtain our petitions, Amen

Lucy met her end as a Christian martyr in the city of Syracuse in Sicily in AD 304, probably as part of the widespread persecution under the Emperor Diocletian. She was named in the list of Roman martyrs and her memory was venerated from a very early date. There is even an ancient inscription naming her in Syracuse itself.

Lucy was raised in a wealthy and pious family, and devoted her life to Christ. Accordingly, she made a secret vow of perpetual virginity. When her father died, Lucy's mother arranged a marriage for her. In order to change her mother's mind, Lucy prayed to Saint Agatha, and eventually her mother was cured of a long-term illness. The marriage was therefore cancelled. Her rejected bridegroom, however, denounced her to the pagan authorities and she was tortured and burned before being killed by a sword thrust in her throat.

St Lucy's name, which suggests light, may have been the reason why she was popularly called upon by the superstitious to ward off eye ailments. In antiquity, failing eyesight was a widespread problem, so a saint who would defend people against the onset of blindness was bound to be popular. In paintings Lucy is often depicted holding one or two eyes in a dish.

St Thomas the Apostle

The name Thomas or Didymus means 'twin'. Thomas was one of the Twelve Apostles, the major disciples of Jesus. The Gospel of St John records four of his sayings, which show him as matter-of-fact, reluctant to believe, but intensely loyal. When Lazarus died and other disciples wanted to persuade Jesus not to risk his life by travelling to Bethany, where the body of Lazarus lay, it was Thomas who intervened. 'Let us go too, so that we might die with him.'

After the Resurrection, it was Thomas – 'Doubting Thomas' – who did not believe that Jesus had risen from the dead. He would only believe if he saw for himself and could touch the wounds made by the nails and the spear. Unlike subsequent doubters, Thomas was given the privilege of proof. He met the risen Jesus and was indeed able to see for himself – and believe.

After Jesus ascended into Heaven, Thomas might have disappeared from history, but for the *Acts of Thomas*, which tell us that the apostles drew lots for the provinces where they were to spread the word about Jesus. Thomas drew India, but objected on the grounds that he was not strong enough and as a Hebrew he would be unable to teach Indians. In a dream he was reassured by Jesus and he eventually agreed to go. The *Acts of Thomas* record that he was eventually martyred at Meliapur and his body was buried in Goa. The Malabar Christians continued long afterwards to regard Thomas as their apostle, and St Francis Xavier found memorials to St Thomas there in his time.

✝ Chronicle ✝

BORN
Not documented

DIED
Died *c*.72 in Meliapour, India from a lance blow at the hands of a pagan priest

PATRONAGE
Architects, blind people, builders, construction workers, geometricians, masons, people in doubt, stone masons, stonecutters, surveyors and theologians

MEMORIAL
3 July – the date when his body was transferred to Edessa in Mesopotamia

PRAYER
O Glorious Saint Thomas, your grief for Jesus was such that it would not let you believe he had risen unless you actually saw him and touched his wounds . . .

St Stephen

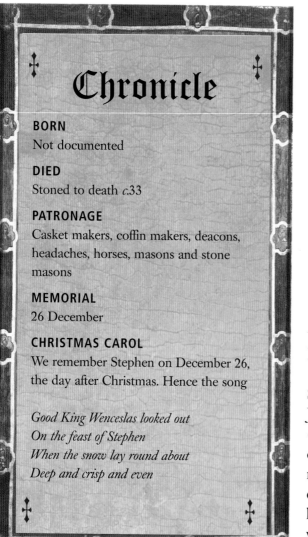

Chronicle

BORN
Not documented

DIED
Stoned to death *c.*33

PATRONAGE
Casket makers, coffin makers, deacons, headaches, horses, masons and stone masons

MEMORIAL
26 December

CHRISTMAS CAROL
We remember Stephen on December 26, the day after Christmas. Hence the song

Good King Wenceslas looked out
On the feast of Stephen
When the snow lay round about
Deep and crisp and even

Stephen was one of seven deacons who were appointed by the Apostles to help in the distribution of charity to the needy. Stephen stood out because of the strength of his faith and his spiritual power. He was a Jew of Greek culture, which enabled him to see Christianity in the wider context of the world outside Israel. It was here that his special 'wisdom' lay.

His preaching led to conflict with traditional Jews. They argued with him, but were unable to outwit him in debate. In the end they seized him and took him to the Sanhedrin for 'speaking against the Temple and the Law'. He looked at the sky and claimed that he could see the glory of God with Jesus himself standing beside God. His accusers rushed at him, dragged him out and stoned him to death for blasphemy. It is not clear whether his execution was legal under Jewish or Roman law; it seems to have been a lynching.

According to an old tradition, the stoning of St Stephen took place outside the Damascus Gate of Jerusalem. In some parts of England, St Stephen's Day (Boxing Day) is also known as wrenning day, after a cruel old custom of stoning wrens on that day in memory of St Stephen. He has the particular distinction of being the very first person, after Christ himself, to have suffered martyrdom for his faith in Christianity. He was celebrated in the middle ages as the first martyr, one of the greatest figures in early Christianity.

St John the Divine

John the Divine was one of the two disciples of John the Baptist, and who on hearing him say, 'Behold the Lamb of God,' immediately followed Jesus to his home. John and his brother James were the sons of Zebedee and Salome. They were evidently men of some means as they had servants – and Salome was among those giving Jesus financial support. The crucial call to become active disciples of Jesus came when, along with their business partners Andrew and Simon Peter, they gave up their fishing boats and nets to follow Jesus.

John, James and Peter belonged to the exclusive inner circle of disciples who witnessed the Transfiguration and were close to Jesus in the Garden of Gethsemane. It was John who asked Jesus to call fire from heaven down on the Samaritans when they refused them shelter. The brothers were themselves full of fire and zeal, and inclined to impetuous and severe solutions. They were given the nickname Boanerges, Sons of Thunder or Sons of Anger, and they appear throughout the Gospel record as fiery Jewish-Christians.

Tradition has it that it was this same John who wrote the Fourth Gospel. The tone of that Gospel seems to be at variance with John the Divine's character, but he was certainly a key witness to the events of Jesus's mission. When news came from the women that Jesus had risen from the dead, John outran Peter to the tomb, and saw that the tomb was empty. John was one of the seven disciples who went fishing on the Sea of Galilee and one of the first to recognise Jesus, risen from the dead, standing on the shore.

Later John was with Peter when the lame man was healed at the Beautiful Gate of the Temple. After that it is uncertain where he went. Tertullian

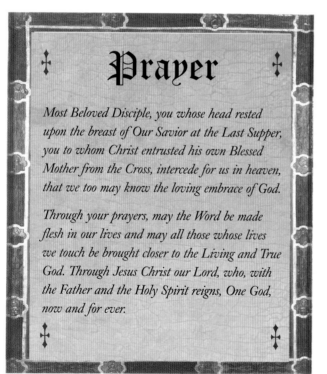

Prayer

Most Beloved Disciple, you whose head rested upon the breast of Our Savior at the Last Supper, you to whom Christ entrusted his own Blessed Mother from the Cross, intercede for us in heaven, that we too may know the loving embrace of God.

Through your prayers, may the Word be made flesh in our lives and may all those whose lives we touch be brought closer to the Living and True God. Through Jesus Christ our Lord, who, with the Father and the Holy Spirit reigns, One God, now and for ever.

writes that he went to Rome and was thrown into a bath of boiling oil, but emerged un-scathed. Eusebius says that in the reign of Domitian John was exiled to the island of Patmos, where he saw the Revelation.

In extreme old age, he amused himself with a pet partridge. When he was criticised for being frivolous, he said, 'The bow cannot always be bent', meaning that everyone has to relax at some time. If he wrote the Gospel, it was towards the end of his life. And if he did, it was probably in part with the intention of correcting a misguided tradition that he was supposed to be the 'disciple that should not die.' The Gospel refers to John as 'the desciple whom Jesus loved'. Both Polycrates and Irenaeus describe John as a high priest, living on into the reign of Trajan and publishing his Gospel in Ephesus; John may have later died at Ephesus.

201

Thomas of Canterbury

Thomas Becket, one of the best known saints of the middle ages, was born in Cheapside in the City of London, the son of Gilbert Becket, a merchant. He was educated at Merton Priory in Surrey, where he acquired the lifelong habits of prayer and self-denial. He also spent some time in the household of Richer de l'Aigle at Pevensey Castle. In the middle ages it was customary for the sons of the rich to acquire manners and independence by living away from home in the castle of some aristocrat, it was the forerunner of the public school system.

Thomas became an accountant and then in 1143 entered the household of Archbishop Theobald of Canterbury, where he gained favour. He was sent away to study Law at Bologna and Auxerre and when he returned to the Archbishop's household he was ordained deacon and made Archdeacon of Canterbury. Only two years after that he was made Chancellor by Henry II, on Theobald's recommendation.

This swift promotion made Thomas the most important man in England after the King and he lived in luxurious style, at least in public, and the King had little idea of the austere churchman he was harbouring as his confidant and friend. Thomas and the King became very close friends. It was commented at the time, 'Never were there two men more of one mind or better friends.'

When Theobald died in 1162, Henry made Thomas Archbishop of Canterbury. Thomas tried in vain to dissuade him, warning that the love between them would turn to bitterest hatred. At the King's insistence, Thomas was ordained priest on one day and consecrated Archbishop the next. Much has been made of the change that came over Thomas Becket at his appointment. Perhaps it was in part that he was taking the job he had been given with appropriate conscientiousness, or rather that he had been a secret churchman all along, and adopted the outward semblance of the courtier for the sake of carrying out his role as Chancellor effectively. Either way, his apparent change of personality and values confused Henry II utterly.

The King intended to reduce the power of the Church in England and make it subordinate to the state, and the first great clash came over the Constitutions of Clarendon. The King claimed that lay (secular) courts should be able to try clergymen who broke the law. Becket refused to agree to this, partly because the punishments introduced by the Norman kings were barbaric and brutal, including blinding and mutilation for minor offences, partly because Becket saw the Church as a useful counterweight to monarchs who seemed likely to become absolute. By creating some immunities, the Church was able to weaken the power of the monarchy.

After a second major confrontation between King and Archbishop at Northampton in 1164, Thomas fled to France, where he appealed to the Pope for support. Eventually the Pope decided in Thomas's favour and King and Archbishop were reconciled. Thomas returned to Canterbury in triumph.

Thomas unwisely refused to absolve the bishops who had disagreed with him, and they complained to the King. In a rage, Henry II famously goaded his knights. It is not certain whether he actively instructed four knights to murder Becket, but it seems likely that he did. They rode in haste to Canterbury with their followers, and found the Archbishop in his palace, taking a meal before going into the cathedral for the evening service.

The monks tried to hurry Thomas into the cathedral where they imagined he would be safe from any violence the knights may have intended. He had just entered the north transept when the knights caught up with him. After an exchange of insults, the knights cut him down with their swords.

The assassination was such a spectacular act of desecration – the Archbishop murdered inside his own cathedral – that it was instantly seen as a martyrdom. The repercussions were felt for centuries. Henry II had to do public penance for his part in the murder. The cult of St Thomas of Canterbury was the greatest single pilgrimage cult of the middle ages, effectively fending off any major take-over by the state in England for over 300 years. It was only when Henry VIII dissolved the monasteries that the monarch succeeded in becoming master of both Church and State. In life Thomas was a powerful and forceful figure, in death he became even more powerful, a monolithic symbol of the fortitude of the Christian Church and its resistance to onslaughts from the secular power.

St Sylvester

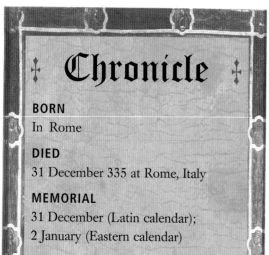

✝ Chronicle ✝

BORN
In Rome

DIED
31 December 335 at Rome, Italy

MEMORIAL
31 December (Latin calendar);
2 January (Eastern calendar)

PAPAL ASCENSION
314

'THE LIFE OF ST SYLVESTER'
by William Caxton, first edition 1483
*Then St Silvester put himself to prayer,
and Saint Peter appeared to him and
said: Go surely to the dragon and the two
priests that be with thee take in thy
company, and when thou shalt come to
him thou shalt say to him in this manner:
Our Lord Jesu Christ which was born of
the Virgin Mary, crucified, buried and
arose, and now sitteth on the right side of
the Father . . .*

ylvester was Bishop of Rome during the reign of the Emperor Constantine the Great, who made Christianity the official religion of the Roman Empire. Some say that Sylvester baptised Constantine, but it is more likely that the emperor was not baptised until he lay dying, by Eusebius, the Arian Bishop of Caesarea.

Sylvester was, nevertheless, Bishop of Rome during a critically important phase in the development of Christianity. It was probably through his influence that Constantine ordered churches to be built in Rome. This in turn may have given rise to the story – almost certainly a fable – that the emperor made the city of Rome over to the papacy on the grounds that the Vicar of Christ (Sylvester himself) should not live in a city that was subject to an earthly ruler. That would have been too much for even a Christian emperor to propose!

Sylvester was too infirm to attend the most important and historic Church council in his lifetime, the Council of Nicaea summoned by Constantine in 325. Because of the large distances involved many key figures were absent. Eusebius the Bishop of Nicomedia was there, as was Athanasius. The Council outlawed the heresy of Arius, which threatened the unity of the Christian Church. A 'Nicene creed' was published to make the nature of Christ's identity clear, and even today is regarded in many churches as the basis of Christian belief. Whether Sylvester's presence at Nicaea would have made any difference to the creed can only be guessed. He died in 335.

INDEX

Quercus Publishing plc
46 Dorset Street
London
W1U 7NB

First published 2006

A catalogue record for this book is available from the British Library.

ISBN 1-905204-25-6

Printed and bound in China.

Picture Acknowledgements
The publishers would like to thank the following for permission to reproduce
photographs: akg-images p.131; Bridgeman Art Library pp.5, 23, 27, 29, 43,
79, 81, 103, 107, 111, 113, 119, 120, 123, 129, 133, 135, 137, 141, 143,
155, 163, 175, 181, 191, 197; Corbis pp.9, 55, 59, 69, 83, 91, 97, 127, 167,
195, 201, 205; E&E Picture Library pp.15, 25, 30, 32, 35, 40, 47, 53, 57,
63, 75, 85, 89, 93, 95, 105, 109, 115, 125, 142, 147, 149, 151, 153, 161,
171, 173, 177, 179, 183, 185, 192; Joanna St Mart Picture Research pp.7, 10,
13, 18, 45, 49, 50, 61, 67, 71, 73, 76, 87, 99, 101, 139, 157, 187, 189, 199, 203;
Mary Evans Picture Library pp.17, 21, 37, 39, 65, 117, 159, 165, 169